THE ART

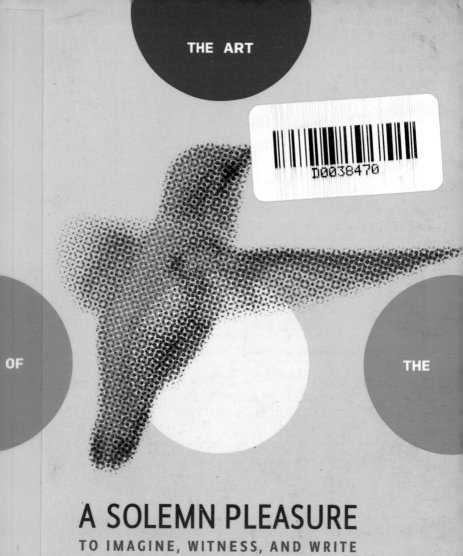

OF

THE

A SOLEMN PLEASURE

TO IMAGINE, WITNESS, AND WRITE

Melissa Pritchard

ESSAY

More Praise for Melissa Pritchard

"Dreamy and delightful." —**NPR's** *All Things Considered*

"Wildly imaginative. . . . Endearingly quirky." —*Glamour*

"Precise and lucid." —*New York Times Book Review*

"Melissa Pritchard has her GPS set to find the *how it is*—out there and in the heart." —**Sven Birkerts**, author of *The Other Walk* and editor of *AGNI*

"Melissa Pritchard's voice is completely her own."
—**Tayari Jones**, author of *Silver Sparrow*

"I have admired Melissa Pritchard's writing for several years now for its wisdom, its humble elegance, and its earthy comedy."
—**Rick Moody**, author of *The Four Fingers of Death* and *On Celestial Music*

"Melissa Pritchard is a treasure." —**Bradford Morrow**, author of *The Diviner's Tale* and *The Forgers*

"Vivid, bold, and wickedly witty." —**Sena Jeter Naslund**, author of *Ahab's Wife* and *The Fountain of St. James Court*

"Melissa Pritchard's prose, that darkly lyrical firmament, is brightened by the dizzy luminous arrangement of her stars and satellites, her great gifts to us: humor, irony, kindness, brilliance."
—**Antonya Nelson**, author of *Bound* and *Funny Once*

"A writer of immense talent." —**Peter Straub**, author of *A Dark Matter*

"No one is quite so brilliant at voicing the all-but-impossible-to-track interior lives of the most complex human beings as is Melissa Pritchard." —**Brad Watson**, author of *The Heaven of Mercury* and *Aliens in the Prime of Their Lives*

A Solemn Pleasure

Also by Melissa Pritchard

FICTION

Spirit Seizures

Phoenix

The Instinct for Bliss

Selene of the Spirits

Disappearing Ingenue:
The Misadventures of Eleanor Stoddard

Late Bloomer

The Odditorium

Palmerino

NONFICTION

Devotedly Virginia: The Life of Virginia Galvin Piper

A Solemn Pleasure

To Imagine, Witness, and Write

Melissa Pritchard

Foreword by
Bret Anthony Johnston

Bellevue Literary Press
New York

THE ART OF THE ESSAY SERIES

A Solemn Pleasure is the inaugural title in Bellevue Literary Press'
The Art of the Essay series, which features compelling, creative nonfiction from
accomplished writers of fiction, demonstrating the Bellevue Literary Press belief
that fine literature knows no boundaries of genre or imagination.

First published in the United States in 2015 by
Bellevue Literary Press, New York

For information, contact:
Bellevue Literary Press
NYU School of Medicine
550 First Avenue
OBV A612
New York, NY 10016

Library of Congress Cataloging-in-Publication Data
is available from the publisher upon request.

Bellevue Literary Press would like to thank all its generous
donors—individuals and foundations—for their support.

Book design and composition by Mulberry Tree Press, Inc.

Manufactured in the United States of America.
First Edition

1 3 5 7 9 8 6 4 2

paperback ISBN: 978-1-934137-96-3
ebook ISBN: 978-1-934137-97-0

For Jillian Robinson

To be a writer is to enter into public life.

—Nadine Gordimer

Contents

Foreword
by Bret Anthony Johnston

Recently, in the Nigerian town of Baga, Boko Haram Islamist militants killed several hundred men, women, and children. Elsewhere, the terrorist group ISIS is regularly recording the beheadings of prisoners and distributing the videos online. An Asian passenger jet has been missing for months and scraps of another were found floating in the Java Sea. In America, there's been a spate of black citizens killed by police, and courts have summarily absolved the officers of any wrongdoing. Ebola has cut a swath through generations in Africa. Shootings in schools, offices, and movie theaters have all made the news while homelessness and hunger tend to garner attention only if a celebrity takes up the cause and shines a light on the issue—often just in time to promote a new film. Note that I haven't mentioned the wars in Afghanistan or Iraq, the ongoing conflict between Israel and Palestine, the widespread allegations of rape on college campuses, what's happening along the Mexican border, or the terrifying flaws in our health care system. There's only so much pain we can bear before numbness sets in and blindness takes over. How fitting, then, that a man begging for pocket change near my office holds up a sign that reads, "I am somebody. Please see. Please help."

In the face of such widespread tragedy, such loss and strife,

why would anyone waste a moment—let alone a lifetime—
writing? (Why, for that matter, would anyone bother reading? Or volunteer to teach or take a class in creative writing?)
The question comes up often enough in a writer's life. Parents
and students, parents *of* students, spouses, parents *of* spouses,
employers, and strangers at public events or on airplanes will
ask it in myriad ways. What they're asking about is indulgence.
The question is important and fair, complex and serious. The
answer, though, is easy. Why write? Why read? Why teach or
study writing? Because story and image, metaphor and syntax,
and the endless combinations of twenty-six letters, confirm our
humanity. These are our defense against apathy, our insurance
against inequality, and ironically, our shelter from indulgence.

The transcendent power of literature, the ways it's made
and shared, the ways it shapes its makers and its believers,
drives this gorgeous and moving collection of essays. Whether
writing about the death of her mother or the horrors of child
slavery, whether the essays explore Ethiopia or the Sudan or
a college classroom, Melissa Pritchard lays bare the soul of a
writer. And in laying bare the writer's soul, she also exposes
the soul of a teacher, a reader, a daughter, and a mother. She
unmasks her fears and vulnerabilities, and she offers her readers the opportunity to lower their own guards, to step beyond
their own comfort zones, to feel those emotions that are all too
handily avoided. Like all great writers, Pritchard has no interest in providing answers. Rather, she strives only to articulate
the questions in a manner that the readers can hear. Her aim is
never to convey information, but only and powerfully to relay
experiences—experiences that are poignant and devastating,
familiar and extraordinary, inspiring and gutting. Individually,
each of these essays confirms that to write is to think and feel,
to take part in the profound and sacred act of witness. Read
together—and the book is so arresting that many readers will

finish it in a single sitting—the essays amount to a clear and irrefutable mandate for empathy.

Which brings me back to that man's sign. *I am somebody. Please see. Please help.* Last semester, I attended a graduate lecture wherein the writer pointed out a quirk of our language: We often use the words "I see" to mean "I understand." So, then, what is the man actually asking of the passersby? To spare some change, yes, but he's also asking for something far more significant. He's asking to be understood, to be seen, to be seen not as homeless but as human because that's what we, his readers, have in common with him, and if we *see* that—if we *understand* how similar we are—then we recognize ourselves in him and his survival becomes our survival. Interesting to note that he's using language, a pristine and semi-poetic phrasing, to grab our attention, and it's equally interesting—though unsurprising—to note that he wants what every writer wants. For his story to matter. For his readers to empathize. For his words to make a difference.

We don't write despite the suffering in the world. We write because of it.

As you read *A Solemn Pleasure*, notice how often you find yourself leaning toward the pages. I did it so often my neck hurt. The pain was minor, but persistent. In fact, this ache—like each of these powerful essays—is still with me. It's a reminder. Each time it flares, I remember one of Pritchard's trenchant sentences. No matter which sentence I recall, it translates to the author beckoning. Look here, she's saying. Come closer. I've got something to show you. Something you need to see.

—Bret Anthony Johnston
Cambridge, MA

A Room in London

F OR TWO MONTHS, in October and November, my official
   address is 38 Falkland Road in Kentish Town, a northern
neighborhood of London. I am a lodger in a long-faced brick
row house common to this area, and though the neighborhood
is considered somewhat rough, the houses themselves, I'm told,
are exorbitantly priced. The house I live in, built over a local
brickworks in the mid-nineteenth century, is narrow and tall;
to reach my room, you must climb four flights of shallow, steep
stairs. On the third landing is a large, uncurtained window
framing a generous vertical portion of English sky, along with a
serrate outcropping of urban London, an unremarkable, calm-
ing view when I pause to catch my breath, stand a moment, and
say softly to myself, London. In a heady rapture over this city,
worn by my own feverish, rapacious explorations, the hunger to
see more, walk further, explore every ancient nook and historic
cranny (a relentless, impossible, enervating ambition), I return
gratefully to my room on Falkland Road, to the diminutive,
lofty refuge where I can retreat, close the squeaking, white wood
door, boil up a cup of tea or cocoa, and retire to read or sleep on
the second dominant piece of furniture in the room, what I can
only, with rueful honesty, call my cot.

The room itself? Another writer's study (I am here while she
is in Canada), furnished primarily with rising planks of books
and a solidly masculine, imposing, tobacco-colored desk. The

room is extraordinarily small. Most new houses in America have walk-in closets as big. I am useless at mental measurement, but I imagine it to be something like nine by six or ten by seven—a giant's shoe box (and I the long shoe), a rectangular, high-ceilinged space, three of its walls painted a matte seafoam green. Open the door, take two steps, and you are at the lummoxish desk, with six tightly packed shelves of another writer's book collection rising above loose papers, manuscripts, and my own rapidly mounting collection of books. Try the door again, look to your left, and half a step away is my cot, my bed of nails, my monastic pallet, my tablet of dreams. It is hard upon the bones, this wafer-thin mattress, covered by a roughly textured military-issue gray blanket, overlaid by a wonderfully warm duvet with a scatter of fuchsia fish, orange tulips, and pink hearts, the sort of pattern chosen by twelve-year-old girls who, ten years ago, aspired to modernity. I have a good feather pillow and two large decorative pillows to prop behind my back; both are lumpy and clad in an abstract African print with angry splashes of orange, blue, and brown. A small side table, a paper lamp, two slender cabinets, set side by soldierly side, one dark green, the other scuffed yellow, each having many small pharmaceutical-like drawers. Follow along to the long clear pane of window, the outside planting box of galvanized tin bursting with yellow and violet pansies, then look down to the surprisingly verdant view of a tiny brick yard as well as a surprise of trees, expanse of sky, and again, the mirage-like suggestion of central London. Along the broad white sill of the window, I have propped postcard portraits of Dickens, Keats, Queen Elizabeth I, and Richard I and II. Nothing matches in this room given over to the reading and writing of books; it is the equivalent of a shed, the bed itself like laying oneself down upon a short stretch of railway track. I can scarcely turn around in this literary nest, there is nothing of decor though decorousness is not absent, and though it is mine, I am not responsible for it. I simply perch. It is homey, with all a writer might want in a refuge: a stereo, an electric boiling pot for the preparation of tea, powdered coffee, or cocoa; and books by the hundreds—seditious, dreamy, dangerously exhilarating, or, in less inspired hours, soporific.

The wall I sleep beside is painted white but covered over, densely scaled with paper sheets, pieces of research for the resident author's latest novel, a book based upon her Romanian relatives. Birth certificates, death certificates, dozens of black-and-white and sepia photographs, a family tree, its curling, withered leaves climbing a solid white trunk of wall. I sleep beneath her Gypsy ancestry, and one night, a photograph of a woman from the turn of the century falls heavily from the wall and lands on my face. Sitting up—was her spirit trying to get my attention, tell me something?—I decide it is quite possible the souls of deceased Romanians could be crowding into this tiny room, that I am not necessarily alone. Dismissing this as a late-night delusion, hemmed in by the dead, by the author's obscure family, paid tribute to in her novel, as well as a row of famous historical figures queued up along the sill, I return to my fitful, living, monkish sleep.

This room with a view, this room of my own, is short-term. In my anchorite's cell, overlooking a sharp haze of London, I have filled a journal with private thoughts and future resolves. I am recovering from the bitter dissolution of a five-year relationship and feel as close as I have ever been to being ten or twelve years old again—adventurous, curious, eager to learn. In the past month, I have been lonely only once, a mood proving both interesting and short-lived. With all of London before me, given a plain lodging and Spartan existence, I savor a feast of epic proportion. In this windowed aerie, with another woman's ancestry on one side of me, and Elizabeth I, Keats, Dickens, and two King Richards on the other, my own life hovers, newly emergent, alert as to who I will become upon leaving this place. The paper lamp casts a benign, autumnal light over my left shoulder as I write, and the morning sun streams in, chasing off a gauzy curtain of mist covering the window. I have paper, a pen, all the books I could read in a year or two's time, and each morning, when I rise from my little cot, my bones momentarily but monstrously ache as I stand barefoot upon a small handmade rug—*Libya*, it says in black woven letters, with two camels, one cream colored, the other darker beige, kneeling, each with its unlikely square eye, facing one another. Libya. Each morning I rise and place bare feet upon this small Middle Eastern rug, a prayer rug, I am told, as a new day, a day of my own, glorious, fraught with the unknown, begins.

Spirit and Vision

I celebrate myself, and sing myself,
And what I assume you shall assume,
For every atom belonging to me as good belongs to you.

—Walt Whitman
"Song of Myself"
1855

I N 1848, WALT WHITMAN was twenty-nine years old and had not published a single text we now remember. He was a political journalist of shrill tone, a radical democrat who had written some extremely bad poems, some dismissible, imitative stories, and a potboiler novel about temperance that sold more in his lifetime than anything else he ever wrote.

Yet seven years later, at the age of thirty-six, this ordinary man with no remarkable talent would publish the most unusual book of poems in English since William Blake's *Marriage of Heaven and Hell*. He published it at his own expense, designed its florid green cover, set the type for it at a friend's printshop in Brooklyn, then convinced America's leading phrenologists to distribute all 795 copies. On the title page, Whitman's name is absent. On the facing page is an engraving of a bearded man in a large hat, standing casually in workman's trousers, and an open shirt collar revealing flannel underwear. To stimulate interest in his book, Walt Whitman wrote a string of anonymous reviews and placed them in magazines.

Whitman's book, with its curious title, *Leaves of Grass*, was published to the same American audience that four years before had refused to read *Moby-Dick* and only one year before had found nothing worth remarking on in *Walden*. Now a middle-aged Brooklyn journalist had fashioned a book few could read or understand—a book met with indifference, bewilderment and disgust, except by Ralph Emerson, who declared it "the most extraordinary piece of wit and wisdom that America has yet contributed," calling it, in fact, the American Poem.

Walt Whitman. A plain, self-educated man, a carpenter's son, schoolmaster, printer, editor, fiction writer, shopkeeper . . . a man who was to concern himself with "the most profound theme that can occupy the mind of man . . . the relation between the (radical, democratic) Me . . . and . . . . Not Me, the whole of the material objective universe," a man who said, "I cannot understand the mystery, but I am always conscious of myself as two—as my soul and I," a man who wrote, in what he called "the language experiment," poems celebrating and honoring anonymous acts of ordinary life. He erased the boundary between life and art, insisting one's life and one's work were the same—so it has always been with saints—and he deeply believed the "soul makes itself visible only through matter."

By 1860, Whitman has attained an eccentric, unsatisfying fame. A cult was developing around him. Some compared him to Christ, some experienced conversions in his presence; reviews of his work were mainly hostile. One reviewer advised him to simply commit suicide. Walt Whitman had violated all the polite norms of his age, and *Leaves of Grass* was on a collision course with conventional literature. He had assaulted the institution of literature, had torn apart language and invented his own. In fact, Whitman laid the groundwork for much modernist writing from Kafka and Beckett to Borges. In 1855, his audacious experiment with language coincided with America's brave experiment with liberty . . . he worked to give the inarticulate and the illiterate their own suffering but lyric voice, and his lifelong religion was a kind of democratic mysticism, with brilliant belief in the individual to act rightly and with inherent goodness in an environment of liberty. For Whitman, God moved and spoke within each of us, and all the physical world was made perfect by divine radiance.

Great writers are witnesses to the spirit of their age. They need not be accepted by their times; they rarely are. Speaking the truth, they may go unheard, be misunderstood or criticized. Later, posthumously, it is said they were ahead of their time.

Walt Whitman died on March 26, 1892, over a century ago. By conventional standards, this man's personal life was a failure. He died penniless, in a small, cluttered room, attended by a few close friends, disciples who understood his genius and future importance. Today the American spirit of industry he so praised has brought us to the edge of ecological collapse, the democratic experiment he believed linked to divinity and human dignity has soured. The bond between self and community, our spirit of social consciousness, is weak and uncertain.

What woman or man, what prophet, is the Whitman of our time?

WHY WRITE? Why add to the tumult of the world? Your competition is fierce . . . from television, film, video, all social media, from the books of other writers living and dead. There currently exists in America an insidious numbness to literature. It is increasingly difficult to publish what is called "literary fiction"; even the best-seller market is not what it was. Stacks of books are returned to warehouses every day, even those blockbuster books publishing houses rely upon to finance more serious, less lucrative books. And how have we, as writers of that literature, become increasingly alienated from the soul of our culture? How have we become so nearly unnecessary? In other parts of the world, to be a writer is to place yourself in physical peril; your words might invite your own death. In other parts of the world, to be a writer is a heroic vocation, for which you may be imprisoned, tortured, "disappeared." On the other hand, thousands of people may assemble to listen to you; as a poet you may be elected to the highest political office. In parts of this world, the power of language is still deeply connected to the soul of the people. Whitman's work was initially met with indifference. By the time of his death he was regarded as a genius and a saint or a derelict and degenerate, depending on your stand. He was in no way dismissible.

We are in danger, I believe, of becoming accustomed to indifference, of being kept within writing workshops, conferences, and seminars where we write and read to a dwindling, closed circle of admirers. Nearly resigned to this peripheral fate, we are then tempted to take ourselves too seriously as far as ego recognition goes, in terms of literary prizes, grants, and publications in journals, yet not seriously enough as essential witnesses to our time. In this decade of environmental trauma and political depletion, when racism has emerged like a virus immune to treatment, when feminism is again under attack and homosexuals newly under siege, I believe in our souls we feel some deep disquiet over this.

A wonderful poet I once heard speak, Francisco X. Alarcón, says that for him, literature is about pain and the healing of that pain. I would also suggest to you that all great literature has an uncreeded and luminous theology behind it.

Before I begin on my idea of art as a form of active prayer, I would like to address the notion of fiction as entertainment. If your desire in writing is to entertain, to be commercially successful, I do think there is a welcome place for writing that is more anodyne, more reliever of pain than healer of that pain. But for many years, I've been moving inexorably toward the concept of literature as sacred vocation, toward Yeats' concept of artists as priests, as shamans, as soul transformers. And perhaps if you are, as I am, aspiring to be this kind of writer (and by this I do not eliminate humor, the power of wit and lightheartedness), you might consider yourselves, however briefly, in the category of holy persons, language saints, saints of storytelling. Many of the tenets of sainthood are also to be cultivated in the committed writer: selflessness, the death of the little self, purity of spirit leading to intensity of vision, a suspension of judgment in regard to your fellow human beings, an intimate acquaintance with ecstasy, sorrow, and revelation. Consider for a moment your work as analogous to intimate prayer in which you address God, and thereby divineness, in all matter.

Some of the things I'm going to talk about I discovered in Aldous Huxley's *The Perennial Philosophy*, and much of what I found in his book is remarkably aligned with Whitman, the transcendentalists, the world of William Blake, George Sand, Annie Dillard, Rilke, Keats, and so many others. We can begin with a metaphysic that recognizes a divine reality substantial to the world of things, lives, and minds, a psychology that finds in the soul something similar to, or even identical with, divine reality, an ethic placing humanity's final end in the knowledge of the immanent and transcendent ground of all being. This is a universal, immemorial idea put forth by all religions, much folklore, and, uncounted times, by great artists. Whitman believed in the poet as agent of transcendent power; he was literal when he referred to his ecstasies, his illuminations.

This divine reality is of such a nature that it cannot be understood directly except by those who choose to fulfill certain conditions, making themselves loving, pure in heart, and rich in spirit. I am talking about mystics, saints, prophets, sages, enlightened ones, the Sufis of Islam, the gurus of India, the Catholic mystics, the Quakers' tradition of inner light that so influenced Walt Whitman, the shamans, and medicine women and men of the Native American tribes. It is from these people and others that we learn of the detachment, charity, and humility essential to being immersed in the one divine reality. It is my assertion that as writers, we bring as many of these same qualities to bear in our work as we possibly can. The idea of the one eternal self within all individual selves, the one divine ground by which all the physical world is pervaded, the notion of each one of us as a vessel for the whole intelligible world, this consciousness, supernatural consciousness, is what transformed Whitman from an ordinary hack writer to a composer of transcendent works, brilliantly cadenced, singing the praises of the divine in all ordinary things, employing sexual imagery to marry spirit with flesh. Enduring literature is suffused with compassion and love. And because we then act in the foolish, vain, mad, self-destructive, and sometimes criminal ways we do, all so characteristically human, this is much of what our stories and poems and novels concern themselves with. And just as the author labors in solitude but is never alone, so the artist, the author, is never poor.

Our one great Promethean labor is to reconcile humanity to itself and to reconnect, through language, humankind to the universe. If we begin with this ambition, then all the techniques, the seminars and workshops to promote confidence and craftsmanship make sense, are valid and valuable.

There is a saying that all poetry, and, I would maintain, all fiction, is about the loss of the Beloved. The Sufi poet Rūmī says the Beloved is all in all, the lover merely veils him, the Beloved is all that lives. Great art addresses this loss, returns us to the Beloved and to a sense of reunion with ourselves.

Ego. Spirit. Separation. Aloneness. Loneliness. Our existence is lived out in this common frustrating state. Created from the brief union of two bodies, born out of another's flesh, we learn to separate—from mother, from family—we become ourselves, we become individuals; then many of us are reabsorbed back into families, our own families, becoming parents ourselves; then the gradual return through the slow natural disintegration of the body to sacred oneness. The circle, and its greater form, the spiral, complete.

All of us have heard stories of people in some shared crisis overcoming difference, working as one to survive some particular trauma. War is an extreme but common example. When our lives are tranquil and undisturbed, we cling to separateness, to our distractions, to our own unique personalities. One peculiarly stubborn Euro-American dream is that of the proud, self-reliant individual, yet look where it has taken us—into profound environmental and societal crisis. This commitment to the self, this cult of the self, has taken us far from Whitman's idea of democracy and community, from the one divine self connected to all individual and equally precious selves.

It is the saint who understands every moment of life as crisis, the crisis of choice between little self and divine self, between personal good and good of the community, between transitory pleasure and infinite bliss. A saint must undertake rigorous training of mind and body just as the soldier must. Yet how simple a soldier's objective—to be courageous, cool-headed, and cooperative enough to kill other human beings he has no personal argument with, people he does not even know.

I would ask you, as writers, to consider your lives a form of perpetual perishing, that as you lose yourselves in devotion and discipline to your work, you will attain the Beloved and begin to perceive the divine reality in all. With spirit informing your vision, may your work become unassailable in its integrity.

Grace Paley, Willa Cather, Nadine Gordimer, and countless others claim that if your commitment isn't to truth, then you are in the wrong line of work. The poetics of silence still exist in America, but as writers I feel we have a responsibility to engage in history, in painful history, to be responsible witnesses to our own time. We are not separate; we are not an indulgent elite. We are not blind to suffering. We are, in fact, aware of our intimate relation to all other beings, and are thus accountable, deeply responsible. We must connect the personal with the political, the political with the spiritual. And though we can only work from our particular place, our given spot in the world, the particular can be a place of great power—the cry of the human heart and the yearning of the human spirit are, after all, universal.

What you have chosen is a profound vocation of healing, and your stories and poems are as sacraments, as visible blessings. Be at the heart and soul of your time, not resigned to what is safe or peripheral. Try to free yourself from attachment to results, to awards, publications, praise, to indifference, rejection, and misunderstanding. Immerse yourself in the common ground of the universe so that your true voice— not the egoistic voice that clamors vainly for power (for it will ruin you if you listen to it)—your authentic voice, supported by sacred reality, may be heard. May your words illuminate your vision, find you compassionate, attuned to human suffering and committed to its alleviation. May truth and its pursuit render your stories and poems and novels of supreme importance in this perilous, inarguably critical time.

Swiftly arose and spread around me the peace and joy and
knowledge that pass all the argument
of the earth,
And I know that the hand of God is the promise
of my own,
And I know that the spirit of God is the brother
of my own,
And that all the men ever born are also my brothers, and
the women my sisters and lovers,
And that a kelson of the creation is love . . .

—"Song of Myself"

1892

How beautiful and perfect are the animals!
How perfect is my soul!
How perfect the earth, and the minutest thing on it!
What is called good is perfect, and what is called sin
is just as perfect . . .

I swear I see now that every thing has an eternal soul!
The trees have, rooted in the ground . . . the weeds of the
sea have . . . the animals

I swear I think there is nothing but immortality!
That the exquisite scheme is for it, and the nebulous float
is for it, and the cohering is for it,
And all preparation is for it . . . and identity is for it . . .
and life and death are for it,

—"To Think of Time"

1855

It is the central urge in every atom . . . To return to its
*   divine source and origin . . .*

—"A Persian Lesson"

1891

To the humanitarian what is home?

—*With Walt Whitman in Camden* by Horace Traubel

1888

From the Deep South
to the Desert South:
An Epiphyte's Confession

CONFESS WHAT I ONCE CONSIDERED my cruelest handicap as a beginning writer—an utter absence of regional voice. My early yearnings to write were blunted by the humiliating sense of having come from no place very dramatic or interesting, no place worth mentioning, at least not for what I considered the elevated purposes of fiction. I was determined to overcome this lack of a regional history, both geographic and societal, by the essentially hopeless decision to cultivate, when imitation palled, as it did after several early stories, a voice colorless as water, a voice so thin in its inflection, so neutral in its rhythms, that it could gather in and reflect all voices, transcribe rich varieties of color and whole species of light. Rather than be defeated by my limitation, I would strive to claim, as my region, the whole world.

I was raised in California, about an hour's drive inland from the Pacific Ocean. My family lived in a suburban ranch-style home. Housing developments are pervasive (some would argue invasive) throughout much of the inhabited West and consist of such architecturally homogenous, low-slung dwellings, each sprawled on perhaps one-half to three-quarters of an acre, each scarcely a ranch but still exhibiting a generous clutch of earth, starkly bulldozed, benignly land-scaped, adapted to human families and small pets rather than to roving herds of longhorn cattle.

I recall my complete confusion one day when asked by my fifth-grade teacher to wear a native costume and bring a bit of ancestral history to class. Along with other classmates, I was asked to provide what should have been easy evidence of my heritage, my ethnic background, the blood from which I had so haplessly sprung. I asked my mother, who answered with vague fondness, recalling a certain French-speaking aunt with a glass eye and a fistful of sour-lemon drops in her black taffeta pocket. Then she remembered, much less fondly, indeed with scarcely contained rage, her Irish father, a salesman, she said, and a liar and a drunk besides. My father proffered even less information as to his side of things . . . there was an allusion to German ancestors who farmed land in central Wisconsin and some mention of a great-grandmother whose singular, if no doubt useful, distinction had been her height—she had been over seven feet tall. There it was—my ancestry, my historic place in the world. When I grew old enough to reflect on such things, I realized my parents had been eager to be rid of ethnicity, of regionalism, of ancestry. For my parents, histories were a social hindrance, a galling brake on progress, progress being marked by a finer car, a bigger ranch house, and an annual membership at the local country club. And since my knowledge of my family history was so sparse, there seemed to be little to be proud of or draw comfort or inspiration or even caution from. Perhaps my parents' intent to ensure me a bland, inoffensive childhood, devoid of the taint of family history, partially explains my feverish response to mid-nine-teenth-century Russian literature and mid-twentieth-century southern literature. In both of these genres, region, or place, is powerfully evoked. Families can be traced back generations, relatives cram into stories, shouting to be heard; here narratives are underscored by a deeply rooted sense of belonging, both geographic and generational. I was as starved for this sense of belonging as I was for the religion vividly demonstrated to me by the Catholic nuns at the convent school I attended. Throughout high school, I, a daughter of agnostics, was more showily religious than any of my classmates, who, born to Catholicism, were bored by it, and like many adolescents, portrayed boredom exquisitely.

Today I can cite among my earliest, most indelible literary influences Leo Tolstoy and Flannery O'Connor. Theirs would be books to commit, were it possible, to memory—for solace, for inspiration, for purest pleasure. The pairing seemed accidental; they were the writers I loved best, their stories heated my blood. So imagine my delight in coming upon an essay by Carson McCullers, from her book *The Mortgaged Heart*, in which she points to strong affinities between mid-nineteenth-century Russian realist and mid-twentieth-century southern regionalist writers. Both, according to McCullers, share a peculiar and intense realism, and circumstances marking southern literature seem strikingly similar to those under which the Russians functioned. A dominant characteristic in both societies was the relative expendability of human life. Both southern and Russian realist writers have been accused of a certain cruelty in their writing. And since horror, violence, madness, murder, and destruction have always been crucial elements in storytelling, what slant of cruelty finds its commonality between these two? McCullers suggests it rises from a technique boldly juxtaposing the tragic with the humorous, the immense with the trivial, the sacred with the bawdy, creating a peculiar, insistent fusion of anguish and farce—the effect upon the reader being one of disturbance, of laughter immediately bitten into by guilt. It is from this intimate alliance of the tragic with the farcical, the first a grand onslaught of emotion undercut by the second, rooted in the mundane, in the homely, in the low detail, that the accusation of cruelty might seem to arise. An absence of proportioned reverence, a missing nimbus of respect around the grieving, no hush around the suffering one, but rather the equivalent of a squawking chicken or a cushion that squeaks offensively as one sits down to address the veiled and somber widow, or a senile old priest babbling of peacocks' tails while he sits beside a woman literally paralyzed by moral guilt. In Tolstoy's novella *The Death of Ivan Ilyich* and in Flannery O'Connor's "The Displaced Person," immense personal disasters are not held sacrosanct from inconsequential or banal happenings. This refusal to grant a kind of hushed frame of privacy around a character's profound realization or epiphany ensures scenes that are both grotesque and comic, and to my way of thinking, stringently, wonderfully true.

The South has always been set apart from the rest of the United States. It has a history all its own, a personality at a remove from the rest of the country. It has neither forgotten nor particularly forgiven its defeat by the North in the nation's civil war. The implications of this, along with the bitter aftermath of defeat, has shaped the southern character in profound ways. There is an economic poverty in the South that outdoes the poverty of any other region. Bitter race and class divisions that still fester are comparable to those that existed in the Russia of Chekhov, Turgenev, Tolstoy, and Dostoyevsky. But the deeper similarity I discovered between these two literary climates was moral passion, a fierce examining of the painful substance of life, a probing of metaphysical and ethical enigmas. Even after his conversion to Christianity, Tolstoy said, "The meaningless absurdity of life—it is the only incontestable knowledge accessible to man." The essentially spiritual underpinning of works by Chekhov, Turgenev,

Tolstoy, and Dostoyevsky is also present in the works of O'Connor, William Faulkner, Eudora Welty, Katherine Anne Porter, and Carson McCullers—who claimed writing was a way of searching for God.

Growing up as I did in an innocuous California suburb, these writers, the southern and the Russian realists, excited me with their exotic, brave, eccentrically couched questions. The very things my parents attempted to shield me from— violence, suffering, poverty, a too distinct ethnic or regional stamp, were the very things I sought out in literature. So it seemed nearly inevitable that when I began to write my own fiction, it was set in nineteenth-century Saint Petersburg and in some hazily defined place I thought of as distinctly southern. There was, I believed, certainly nothing worth writing about in my neighborhood. I could claim no place, no region, no rich history out of which to write. All I could hope to do in those early days was to emulate writers I admired. I pitied my own rootlessness, felt like a fake, an imposter. I saw my characters' voices as tricked out in other people's tongues. I feared I was not much more than a clever mimic.

In all regions of the South, raconteurs abound; southerners are famous for their ability to enthrall with anecdotes and humorous stories. Anecdote, for credibility, relies upon memory, and memory is affixed to specific history. I learned this firsthand from a graduate school roommate with whom I became good friends. She was from South Carolina, and while modestly insisting she was no storyteller, not at all, not like her uncle Yancy for instance, she kept me happily awake for hours at night, recounting tale after tale about her family members, most of whom had lived in the same neighborhood for generations. When my sister moved with her husband to the South, she found everyone's first question upon meeting her to be about the origins of her family, who was she related to that they might possibly know? Here was a precisely calibrated and maintained social register . . . and if, like my sister, you could claim no pedigree—because over at the other end of the country, where you were from, the West, you were expected to disregard family in order to re-create yourself—then to answer, as my sister did, with only the sketchiest knowledge of your past was clear and shocking indication of some hidden disgrace, some horrific and secret family scandal. In the South, your family, your place of origin, is either a means of social ascent or a hard-to-overcome stasis or even descent. Moral cautions abound in anecdotes of family; one's beginnings are both instructive and confining. Perhaps one of the deeper impulses of those who moved West was the desire to nullify the past, to start again, to have no traceable "roots" and to be able to reinvent themselves without history, to theologically invest in the notion of free will and autonomy over notions of fatalism and predestination.

I returned to my elementary school the next morning and in a quavering voice sang the French nursery rhyme "Frère Jacques." I wore a black dress with a flowery print my mother insisted "looked French," and I talked a good deal about my dog, George, a dachshund, a small hunting dog of German origin. Yet I was no more deficient than my other classmates in the patchy sort of ethnic evidence I brought into class that day. My rootless situation was usual. This was, after all, California—the sandy, eroding edge of a continent. My younger daughter came home with a similar assignment around the same age, to bring a dish of food representing her place of ancestry. We struggled through a cookbook or two and came up with an easy recipe for Irish soda bread. Meanwhile, in some perverse nod to tradition, I told her all about her grandmother's French-speaking aunt with the glass eye and pocketful of lemon drops. I described her great-grandfather, the Irish salesman. Being a writer, I embellished what little I knew with speculation and fanciful detail, desiring, I suppose, to give my daughter more than I had been given of my origin.

All this can be boiled down into what I call an epiphyte's confession. At the Desert Botanical Garden near my home in Arizona, there is a display of these desert plants. Epiphytes require practically no soil in order to thrive as their root system is above ground. They are considered parasitic, sometimes living on other plants or on rock ledges, wherever they find a hospitable foothold. These days I no longer feel a deficiency of locale, nor do I yearn to be a southern writer nor to be writing back in nineteenth-century Russia, as I once did. I have lived in the Midwest, the West, and the Southwest, and though I have had stories published in anthologies called *Women Writers of the Southwest* and *Best of the West*, I remain unconvinced I am any more of a western writer than I am a southwestern or midwestern writer. I resist the very categorization I once felt deprived of and believed to be a stony impediment to my becoming a "real" writer. Yet even as I disclaim influence, I realize one collection of my stories, *The Instinct for Bliss*, is thoroughly influenced by my life in the West and Southwest. I think of Flannery O'Connor, William Faulkner, and Eudora Welty, southerners who wrote out of regions they grew up in or lived in, and know I may always envy such writers, whose fictional characters are possessed of destinies inextricably linked to place, just as I once envied my convent classmates their Catholicism. Oh, to belong!—to have generational history and connections beyond oneself, rather than the free-floating, anxious liberty my parents, with well-meaning intent, bequeathed me. Many of my stories concern characters who have no strongly defined sense of place, who encounter other characters living inside of, even confined by, boundaries of culture and family. My characters blunder in, try to assimilate, fail in tragicomic ways, stir up all sorts of trouble as they misinterpret, overidealize, underestimate. The character who yearns to belong but is fundamentally incapable, both by temperament and by training, of truly belonging . . . this character, a parable of myself, announces herself again and again in my fiction.

With defensive pride, I once claimed I had no attachment to place, that my writing would attain emotional significance despite the deprivation of region. I struck an attitude of insouciance, bravado, indifference. Gradually, I have come to believe I can have the best of both worlds, one defined, the other emptied out, waiting to be invented. I was given a thin veneer of specific culture along with a rootless freedom, and through writing fiction, I attempt to see if and how such a life can be sustained.

Not long ago, I was flying into San Francisco after having been away from California for years. From the window of the plane, I looked down on the dry, rolling foothills, a dark gold expanse of land I couldn't recall assimilating in any emotional way, and no one could have been more astonished that I to find myself weeping, overcome with unsought emotion, the single word *home* repeating itself, reverberating within me. In some way I had not fully understood, my flesh was indelibly marked by the land I grew up in, marked even by the suburb I revisited on that trip, by the houses I had grown up in, as I, in each case, experienced the same uprush of emotion. These ranch houses, built in the fifties, were brave, naive proclamations of middle-class safety and order, of a hoped-for affluence and democratic peace. Contemporary American fiction has been criticized by critics like John W. Aldridge in his book *Talents and Technicians* as having no sense of place; if used at all, Aldridge argues, place functions as a meaningless, neutral backdrop. There is no distinct geography, no sense of region in the work of modern writers, Aldridge claims, no history—and without history, there can be no memory, and without memory there can be no sense of emotional connection in the narrative. A consequent absence of meaning, camouflaged by brilliant stylistic technique, lies at the colorless and hollow heart of much contemporary American fiction. I find Aldridge's argument compelling but would deflect the blame from geography, from the transience of American culture so aptly symbolized by that mobile nest, the car, and say instead that I think many American writers are afraid to look into the future, because the future as place is too ominous to think about, and that a profound disillusionment, a gnawing sense that meaning no longer has the power it once did to effect change, may have rendered contemporary writers enamellers of despair.

The desert Southwest, where I now live, is fast becoming overpopulated, a kind of overcolonized utopia for disenchanted easterners. The desert has always been a place of migration, of transience and rootlessness, of searching and reinvention. There is an exhilaration unto madness that affects people when they first arrive here. Vast, untrammeled expanses of space, horizons that stretch forever, skies that billow out eternally— one's whole sense of proportion shudders and shifts. When my husband and I separated, not long after we had moved to northern New Mexico in 1986, we were informed by our marriage counselor that he saw this sort of thing all the time . . . nothing was more common, he said, than a family or couple moving to the Southwest to get away from the press of business, the obligations of relatives, the crowded spaces and calendars, than divorce. With the bands of civilization loosened, people tended to experience anxiety coupled with reckless release, and this in turn produced a particular brand of honesty . . . confessions of I don't love you anymore, haven't for years, I feel myself changing, I need to find out who I really am, can't very well do that with you—reminder and living reproach from my old false life—countless marriages, the counselor informed us, crack under the influence of wide open spaces.

Many American artists, particularly women, have unexpectedly found authentic voices in the Southwest desert. Freed from patriarchal constraints and societal conventions, the very qualities that work to hold marriages together, freedom has liberated a great many women artists—Willa Cather, Georgia O'Keeffe, Mary Austin, among others. Before I moved to the Southwest, I had been living in a conservative area of the Midwest, trying earnestly to be a good wife and mother as well as a writer. Arriving in Taos, New Mexico, two unexpected events occurred. With traditions and obligations lifted and expectations abated, I found I could breathe. I felt a different self emerge from deep inside me, a creature akin to the girl I had been at ten, eleven, and twelve—adventurous, high spirited, curious. I came to know a little about Hispanic culture, about that tightly knit group of people of mixed Indian and Spanish heritage who have a deep love of the land and a deep connection to family and religion. This proved a potent combination, an irresistible lure for me, just as had the Russians in their literature and southern writers in theirs. I fell in doomed love with a Hispanic man. All of this was precipitous and uncontemplated . . . and years later, I easily see that most of my attraction to him was a response to his love of the land he had grown up on, his closeness to his family and to his religion, and above all, his unabashed emotion for these things . . . exactly what I, as a child, had never known.

This longing for what I never had has finally been balanced by a necessary pragmatism. I cannot change who I am. I have had ample opportunity to witness the limiting constraints imposed on an individual by generations-old ties to land and family. I recognize the disadvantages of place, helping me to deromanticize its value. As a writer, I accept what my parents gave me, not as the social advantage they hoped I would claim, but from a perspective as the perpetual outsider, which, for a fiction writer, is not a bad position—to be the detached observer who sees what others, more deeply rooted, cannot. There has been an erosion of that wistful, imitative voice of the young writer I once was, and a strong sense of opposite advantage, an awareness that I can speak as I please, watch, observe, listen, record, and define my own legitimate sense of space—I can claim the identity of the transient, the migrant, the epiphyte. I see now that no place is still a firm place, and that displacement can be its own region. I can compare myself to that other famous southwestern desert plant, the tumbleweed, which easily releases from its roots to roll unhindered across the arid landscape. I am not alone or unique in this comparison; there are many contemporary American writers of the tumbleweed or epiphyte variety. Botanists know the tumbleweed as a harbinger plant that arrives in an area only when the land has been so traumatized, so overgrazed and depleted, that little else can grow. It appears when there's trouble in the soil. Maybe my sort of writer is inspired to write when there's trouble, deep trouble, in the human landscape.

Today, in a gentle irony, I live in a ranch-style home in a suburban development near the university where I teach. My lush, irrigated yard has citrus and palm trees, scarlet bougainvillea, and even the full-blown rose hedges I remember from my California childhood. Near the end of their lives, each of my parents began to speak a great deal about the past, telling stories about long-dead relatives. I learned I am related to Wild Bill Hickok, that one of my relatives, a professor at the University of Dublin, eloped with a young woman and immigrated to the United States. One of my German relatives started his own religion in the middle of the prairie grasslands, another was a prosperous mortician. I gather in this faded bouquet of relations, find connections long after I had ceased longing for them. All this adds increase, not justification, to my work. As a writer, I emerge from a wistful emulation of the South to new forms of expression in the desert Southwest and find myself thankful for all that has come my way, whether by way of liberty to invent or by specific connection to place and people; all of it has been put to use, all of it a gift of voice, fiction's voice, speaking, at its finest, for the human heart and encompassing, with fleeting precision, all the world.

On Kaspar Hauser

I N THE AUTUMN OF 2004, I took up brief residence in London's
British Library to research and write a story about the nineteenth-century German child prisoner, Kaspar Hauser. The
story was originally inspired by Jeffrey Masson's book *The Wild
Child*, an account of Kaspar Hauser's captivity in a dungeon,
his quick, cruel fame and tragic end. In the cloistered hush of
a library containing over thirteen million books and a world-
renowned collection of rare manuscripts, I floated words in
black ink across thick white pages and composed fifteen drafts
of "The Hauser Variations." Seated at a plain, illumined desk,
I wrote about a German boy kept barely alive in an earthen
grave, his only companion a tiny, white wooden horse.

In London for an academic term, I was teaching a creative
writing class at Warwick University in Coventry. On Tuesdays,
I took the train to Warwick from Euston Station, taught my
class, and returned to London by train on Wednesday afternoons. All other days of the week belonged to me, and I spent
them walking the city, exploring its museums, cathedrals,
galleries, theaters, parks. But when I walked into the British
Library one afternoon, I knew I had found the perfect setting in
which to write my story about Kaspar Hauser. Every morning,
as soon as the library opened, I would show my reader's pass,
shove my coat, scarf, purse, and umbrella into a small locker,
and gladly divest myself of the wrangling, noisy world. With

a pen, sketchbook, and a little money for lunch, I would seek out a congenial desk, switch on its small brass lamp, and enter the sad, strangely beautiful world of Kaspar Hauser. A feral child, exposed to unkind notoriety, Kaspar had had a gentle nature. He drew flowers and butterflies; he marveled at constellations in the night sky. Since his murder in an orangery by an unknown assassin, speculations about young Kaspar Hauser's true identity have inspired countless films, poems, and stories.

I brought some of my own research notes, but requested additional books from the librarians, collections of early nineteenth-century German lieder, or folk songs, hymns, books on Freudian theory. Every day, at a certain noon-ish hour, I would take my black sketchbook, seek out the library's café, drink strong black tea and eat warm scones with clotted cream and jam while editing my morning's work. It didn't take long before my ballooning waistline betrayed my weakness for raisin-studded pastries. Part of the experiment, I rationalized. Scones and ink.

Rules in the British Library were strictly enforced; everyone around me appeared to be seized by some passionate, bookish endeavor. So rigid was the library's code of conduct, its adherence to order, that if a person should die at his desk, he was to be left there until after closing time so as not to disturb anyone still breathing and laboring nearby. In my new and temporary home, the pursuit of knowledge, the art of scholarship, proved superior to the inconvenience of death.

In December, I left London, the final handwritten draft of "The Hauser Variations" in my suitcase. I was curious to see what my experiment in paper, ink, and a scones-and-cream diet had wrought, and had no clear opinion of the story's merit beyond the blissful hours I had spent writing it. Typing up the manuscript, I submitted it to *Conjunctions*; five days later, the editor, Bradford Morrow, called, wanting the story for his next issue.

Even now, when I think of "The Hauser Variations," I remember sitting at a wooden desk among ordered rows of identical desks, the dominant sound that of the pages of books being turned. Warmed more by my little lamp than by the sun's rays streaming whitely, coolly, down from high windows, I remember the sober-faced librarians, acolytes at their stations, the uniformed guards checking, with brief, polite respect, one's pass and books. At closing time, I collected my things from my locker and exited, one among hundreds of other dark-coated, book-loving souls, into London's rainy darkness, and headed to the station, my sketchbook sheltered inside my coat. I felt part of some great congregation of worshippers—readers, scholars, and writers with common-held faith in printed, bound knowledge. And sometimes, I thought of those thirteen million books, of all the ancient manuscripts shrouded inside the library's vast, locked, and galleried night, and wished I could hear the low murmuring of their authors, separated and ranked, some imprisoned in locked glass cases. I regarded these books as devotional objects, as inked and holy histories, reliquaries of the human mind.

How utterly absorbed I was, those weeks in the British Library, researching and writing a German child's haunting tale. Content in my purposeful solitude, surrounded by companionable souls, a few living, most dead, and multitudes more, a near infinity of characters and historical figures richly conjured, steadfastly preserved.

Time and Biology:
On the Threshold of the Sacred

*It is the courage to make a clean breast of it in the face of
every question that makes the philosopher. He must be like
Sophocles' Oedipus, who, seeking enlightenment concern-
ing his terrible fate, pursues his indefatigable enquiry, even
when he divines that appalling horror awaits him in the
answer. But most of us carry in our heart the Jocasta who
begs Oedipus for God's sake not to inquire further.*

—Schopenhauer to Goethe
November 1819

I. Time and Biology: On the Threshold of the Sacred

WILLIAM FAULKNER ONCE SAID writers are people obsessed with
time. Time, as we live within its boundaries, is severely limiting, a lesser aspect of injustice. Here I refer to linear, sequential
Newtonian time, not the more complex, singularly fluid nature
of Einsteinian time. As the medium through which we move,
time is the illusion we feel most ensnared by. The past, barring
our largely unreliable remembrance of it, is irretrievable, and
the future vulnerable to conditions of chance. If past actions can
condemn or exonerate us, events in our future are anguishingly
unglimpsed. In an almost cruel equation, time equals fate.

We are understandably eager, then, to comprehend current, more liberating theories of time and space. Each of us, in rare moments of release, has experienced freedom from the ligatures of hours, minutes, days. Our common lives are played out in a straightforward-seeming fashion. The mathematical system has been long agreed upon, clock and calendar remain the organizing principles of secular society. Cause and effect still hold sway, though how anxiously, how hopefully, we intuit and find confirmed in both physics and metaphysics the illusory nature of this linear grid work of time.

I once took my children to see the famous illusionist David Copperfield. His tricks, his magic sleights of hand—and body—were marvelously clever, but it was his last illusion, interestingly enough performed within the context of a story wherein a small boy encounters his grown self, a magical space where child and adult exist simultaneously, a simple but poignant enactment, that I witnessed in the audience as it rose up, applauding, and felt in myself, as part of that audience, humanity's bittersweet yearning for a miracle, longing for release from all structures of time and mortality. In literature, this yearning is expressed again and again in infinite variety: stories of awakening, of journeys, of strangers bringing deliverance from the ordinary, tales of adventure and escape, of transcendence and transformation, of descent into liberation (here I refer to Heracleitus' notion of downward release, popular with gothic and romantic writers, wherein a character embarks upon a downward spiral of willed degeneration and dissolution of self, finding release much the way a mystic, through abstinence and self-denial, seeks to be free of the self).

A second immutable restriction, a grand scale injustice, can be found in biology. The superbly complex entrapment in fleshy form, by its very nature, implies mortality, the cessation of specific, individual forms and the perpetual, extravagant re-creation of others. The myriad ingenious ways humans seek to deny mortality play out in literature. I think of Gustav von Aschenbach's deadly obsession with the young Polish boy, Tadzio, in Thomas Mann's *Death in Venice*, of Ivan Ilyich's denial of the seriousness of his illness in Tolstoy's *Death of Ivan Ilyich*—obsessive, doomed attempts to commute the sentence of death. Stories illustrating such mortal chafing can readily be found.

It is chiefly through the enactment of ritual and ceremony, whether public or private, self-generated or grounded in tradition, that we seek to cross the threshold of limitation, move out of the profane restraints of time and biology into a more sacred, perhaps immortal space. Through ritualized ceremony, calling upon magic, exhorting numerous divinities, and through certain ways of practicing the artistic process, we attain tenuous liberation.

The sort of art I am most interested in creating takes as inspiration Yeats' notion of the poet as shaman, of the writer taking upon her shoulders the burden or mantle once worn by priests and priestesses. And if writers are, as Doris Lessing claims, architects of the soul, and if language is made entirely of vibration, and if some vibratory patterns are more radiant, more archetypally true than others, then to cross that threshold into the sacred, to hope to become that sort of story artist, one must begin to pursue, or at least consider, the gift of anonymity.

II. Anonymity: The Bliss of the Impersonal

The thirteenth-century poet Rūmī said all poetry is about the loss of the Beloved, and I believe loss leads the artist to her truest work. Each of us comes into the world naked and empty handed, each will leave the same way. Human life is predicated upon cumulative loss; accompanying loss is yearning for reunion, and hidden within that yearning, the instinctual awareness that to achieve the bliss of reunion with the

Beloved, one must surrender the small self, the ego, the husk that protects us yet would have us believe it is all there is, all we are. As Thomas Merton, the contemplative mystic and poet, said in a letter to James Baldwin in 1963, "At the heart of the matter then is man's contempt for truth, and the substitution of his 'self' for reality." This limited self, much like the illusions of linear time and finite matter, would bind us within its commands and urgencies, its seductive raptures and burgeoning woes. We seek our way out of this third restraint, this third injustice, the narrow cabinet of self. Whether through erotic passion, chivalric love, hedonism, self-mortification, or mysticism, whether through the path of intoxication or license, forms of fanaticism, or the path of *dharma*, devoted and selfless service to others, we struggle to free ourselves from the small, cordoned off, solitary chrysalis of self. We ache, all of us, for a miracle.

Simone Weil, the French religious thinker, poet, political activist, and philosopher, spoke of the artist's "sacred anonymity." It is dangerously false, she thought, to attach too much importance to personality in one's art. Imagine, for a moment, laying no claim to your work. The Shakers believe they receive their arts as gifts from the spiritual world. Persons who strive as artists of any kind are said to be laboring for a gift and are called instruments; it is forbidden the artist be known to anyone but a few church elders. Imagine, if you will, laying no claim to your work, laboring for a gift. Willa Cather once remarked that the truest happiness came from losing oneself in something greater than oneself. And Emily Brontë: "If I could, I would always work in silence and obscurity, and let my efforts be known by their results." In his lecture on literary ethics given in 1838, Emerson, who, near the end of his writing career, referred to the "infinitude of the private man," said, "Let the youth [here he refers to the scholar/poet] study the uses of solitude and of society. Let him use both, not serve either. The reason why an ingenious soul shuns society, is to the end of finding society. It repudiates the false, out of love of the true." Of the Irish writer William Trevor, his friend Pat O'Connor says, "He's a private man. He finds the pursuit of glory and fame fairly horrendous. In crowds of people, he's utterly charming but he's always looking for the door. He wants an escape route nearby." "Actually," Trevor says, "I don't think I believe that as a writer I belong in society at all. I think writers, any artists, belong outside, on the edge, looking in. Because society is after all, our meat; society is what we comment on in some way. In order to write about people, you have got actually to stand back quite a distance. In a room full of people I feel very shy and want to get back into the shadows. The shadows are where I think I belong."

I believe there are two discernible paths to anonymity, to this setting aside of the socialized, conventional self in order to better connect with humanity in one's art. One is suffering, the other compassion. Predicated upon loss, the human condition evokes suffering. One can either embrace it, an unfashionable ideal, hugely unappealing to most of us, or wait one's turn, in a kind of suppressed dread, wait to be sought out, await the unannounced suffering for which one is never prepared and always surprised by. Suffering, said Teresa of Avila, is the swiftest route to the Beloved, and affliction, believed Simone Weil, the mark of humanity. Abandoning oneself to the crucible of suffering (no easy task, both biology and ego resist) or forced to it by inevitable circumstance, we come by degrees to nonattachment, to letting go of concerns over gains or losses, temporal triumphs or defeats. For those thus far spared suffering, surrender to affliction, any willed flensing of the self, seems an affront; it terrifies and frightens. Yet for the artist, this may prove a crucial phase to pass through. In one film adaptation of Louisa May Alcott's autobiographical novel *Little Women*, the German professor says of Jo's first novel, it is not written from your heart, it is not written from your soul, when you have courage enough to write truthfully, then your work will be worthy of you. It is not until her younger sister Beth dies that Jo, through tremendous grief, is released into the gift of true creativity. Out of an inferno of suffering, Jo March forges a timeless work. To ignore the redemptive value of suffering is offence, what Plato would call the lie of the soul. To acknowledge suffering as necessity's gift to human mortality, and rather than resist or deny or argue with it, to surrender, is to come near Schopenhauer's notion of compassion as a kind of willed renunciation of the ego, an emptying of the self.

I think here of Thom Jones' short story "The Pugilist at Rest," of his character who jabs and boxes his way through life, until, in both a forced and willed surrender to it, he achieves a self-deprecating, radiant melancholy, a heartrending sublimity.

I think of Chekhov's stories, and of Gogol's "The Overcoat," so clever, so superbly witty, yet at its source is an observer very much like the recording angel of God, who sees with a non-judgmental, compassionate eye.

Compassion, that "sweetest sympathy," is, for the artist, a second way out of the finite self. Here it helps to think in terms of writing from the authentic voice as distinct from the voice of personality. When one writes from what Simone Weil referred to as "the genius voice" and not from the narrower voice of personality, one becomes anchored in a place of truthfulness. "Artistic growth," Willa Cather said, "is, more than it is anything else, a refining of the sense of truthfulness. The stupid believe that to be truthful is easy; only the artist, the great artist, knows how difficult it is." "The Pugilist at Rest" is a work blazing with the force of authentic voice. In an interview, Thom Jones said that for years he wrote to please other people (the voice of personality). "The Pugilist at Rest" was the first story that he wrote because he wanted to, because he had to (the voice of authenticity). More than other stories I assign students to read, Jones' has the most consistently powerful effect, causing them to look upon literature with wholly new respect. Suddenly, literature matters.

Writing out of our easily accessible, politely socialized personalities, we risk joining the cult of personality. No matter how clever our way with language or how brilliant our intellect, we risk shallowness, risk becoming dependent upon definitions of public taste. One has only to read the biographies of Herman Melville, Emily Dickinson, Walt Whitman, among countless others, to realize that genius and public recognition do not rely upon each other, that public acclaim is no proof of genius. In the *New Yorker* article on William Trevor I quoted from earlier, the interviewer, Stephen Schiff, says,

> Crazy artists, or flamboyant ones, can be strangely comforting. We feel we understand where their visions come from; we're lulled by the symmetry of turbulent art and turbulent lives. But what about those other, more enigmatic figures, the placid and the sane, the middle-class, burgher like souls who betray no evidence of the visionary within until they apply paint to canvas—or pen to paper, like Trevor? "At cocktail parties and things," Trevor says, "people tell me, 'I don't know how someone like you can write the terribly gloomy things you write.' And the answer is that you become a different person as soon as you sit down at the typewriter. I'm very much against the notion that the person and the writer are the same. There's no need for a man to show his creativity. There's nothing to show."

How does one approach the hidden, authentic voice? By disciplined waiting, by reverent listening. To encourage students to listen at this deeper level, I have them ask themselves one question: If I have only three months to live and one story to write, what will that story be? It is a simple exercise in surrender that, surprisingly, works. Stories rising from this focal point move to a deeper level. When students, trained to camouflage themselves in academic rhetoric, to shun emotion, to not speak of the yearnings of the soul, begin to listen, they stop writing to please others. As so beautifully stated in Octavio Paz's introduction to Elena Poniatowska's *Massacre in Mexico*: "For the chronicler of an era, knowing how to listen is even more important than knowing how to write or better: The art of writing implies previous mastery of the art of listening. A subtle and difficult art, for it requires not only sharp ears, but also great moral sensitivity, recognizing, accepting, the existence of others."

When authentic existence and art are conjoined, when one's life begins to consecrate the lives of others, here is the point where we cross the threshold into the impersonal and enter that sacred anonymity where all art addresses the loss of the Beloved, the yearning for reunion, where the Beloved and the artist, as Lover, reflect, reveal, and become each other.

To create from this place, to remain here, requires, beyond patient listening, the cultivation of courage.

III. Courage: The Artist as Witness

If, as John Gardner asserts in his book *On Moral Fiction*, true art is moral, if art instructs by seeking to improve life, then the artist finds herself, as Simone Weil insists, accountable. She must be conscious of what she espouses. To be accountable to the power of language and responsible at least for the conscious intent of one's stories demands courage on the part of the artist.

And courage, as I think about it, seems to have something to do with the willingness to eternally, doggedly pursue truth, no matter what the threat to our safe notion of things.

An almost intolerable tension exists between the mind's sense of its own eternity and the anguished awareness of life's mortality. To be capable of sustaining this tension, the artist must cultivate Keats' "capacity for a negative genius," a capacity to tolerate, endure, even thrive on uncertainty, to be capable of posing, as Chekhov claimed we must, the correct questions and not impose answers. To go where narrative events prove most dangerous, where the risk to the integrity of one's characters is highest, to refer not to secular laws of justice so much as to examine their disturbing exceptions demands courage. As Émile Zola said in "J'Accuse," "I have but one passion, the passion for the light, in the name of humanity which has suffered so much and which is entitled to happiness . . ."

We are in an age of extremes and exaggerations, poised between the psychic toxicity of two world wars and the unrelieved threat of global extinction. There are at least forty wars raging in the world today, and as we find ourselves bathed in a sickly green light of apocalyptic fever (in a recent poll, 60 percent of Americans believe the end of the world is close at hand), I suggest that, as writers, we strive to be witnesses to the events of recent history, that we be willing to give testimony in the face of whatever lies before us.

For specific example, I look to Albert Camus' *The Plague*, a novel bearing literary witness to the Holocaust. Camus said in his Nobel Prize acceptance speech, "The writer's function is not without its arduous duties. By definition, he cannot serve today those who make history; he must serve those who are subject to it." Published in 1947, *The Plague*, relating the story of a town stricken down by bubonic plague, is an allegory of the struggle against Nazism. It is interesting to note that Camus was a member of the French Resistance, that he edited the French underground newspaper *Combat*, and that a long extract from *The Plague* appeared clandestinely in occupied France in a collection of resistance texts. One could say then that his novel was initially produced as underground testimony, as an action of verbal resistance, not as a simple description of conflict, but as an actual intervention in that conflict. The literature of testimony is not an art of leisure but an act of urgency, and in Camus' conception, must be in a state of constant obligation.

In an editorial for *Combat*, he wrote,

> It is true that consciousness is always lagging behind reality ... The world has changed far more in the past fifty years than it did in the previous two hundred years ...

And in his 1959 lecture "Create Dangerously"

> To tell the truth, it is not easy, and I can understand why artists regret their former comfort ... Indeed, history's amphitheater has always contained the martyr and the lion. The former relied on eternal consolations and the latter on raw historical meat. But until now the artist was on the sidelines. He used to sing purposely, to encourage the martyr and make the lion forget his appetite. But now the artist is in the amphitheater. Of necessity, his voice is not quite the same; it is not nearly so firm.
>
> It is easy to see all that art can lose from such a constant obligation. Ease, to begin with, and that divine liberty so apparent in the work of Mozart. It is easier to understand why our works of art have a drawn, set look and why they collapse so suddenly. It is obvious why we have more journalists than creative writers. The period of the revered master, of the artist with a camellia in

his buttonhole, of the armchair genius is over. To create today is to create dangerously. Any publication is an act, and that act exposes one to the passions of an age that forgives nothing.

The problem is more complex, as soon as it becomes apparent that the battle is waged within the artist himself. The doubt felt by the artists who preceded us concerned their own talent. The doubt felt by artists of today concerns the necessity of their art . . . the questioning of art by the artist has many reasons . . . among the best explanations is the feeling the contemporary artist has of lying or of indulging in useless words if he pays no attention to history's woes.

Simone Weil, a contemporary of Camus whom he greatly admired (saying she had a madness for the truth) believed the whole object of love and justice was what she named *Malheur,* that woe that penetrated the soul's innocent depths, causing it to cry out, Why am I being harmed? For Weil, this was the most important question in human history: It is history itself— to admit the truth of *Malheur* with no assurance of consolation or solution or neat equation, with no reassurance we will be saved—to pose this in one's fiction, requires courage. We find ourselves, if not today, then soon enough, in the amphitheater.

And lastly, to admit the necessity of evil, evil being that which obstructs the good, that which diminishes joy, demands no small degree of valor. To examine, in the context of fiction, ambiguous moral questions—am I doing good, am I doing harm?, the notion of unintentionality, the fragile nature of moral goodness, the notion of tragedy as a critique of virtue when virtuous action on the part of the protagonist proves harmful . . . to pursue these sticky sorts of moral equations in one's work demands courage. How much force of accident or chance can a character sustain and still maintain her integrity, the precious ideal of herself? Part of the peculiar beauty of human excellence is its vulnerability. Greek tragedies are full of good people ruined by the accident of uncontrolled events. Even more disturbing in these tragedies are good people who undertake bad actions, presumably to attain a higher good. One of the real sources of terror in life is to realize that everyone has his or her justification.

In speaking of his own work, Henry James said,

> No themes are so human as those that reflect for us, out of the confusion of life, the close connection of bliss and bale, of the things that help with the things that hurt, so dangling before us forever that bright hard medal, of so strange an alloy, one face of which is somebody's right and ease and the other somebody's pain and wrong. To live with all intensity and perplexity and felicity in its terribly mixed little world would thus be part of my interesting small mortal; bringing people together who would be at least more correctly separate; keeping people separate who would be at least more correctly together; flourishing, to a degree, at the cost of many conventions and proprieties, even decencies; really, keeping the torch of virtue alive in an air tending infinitely to smother it; really, in short, making confusion worse confounded by drawing some stray fragrance of an ideal across the scent of selfishness, by sowing on barren strands, through the mere fact of presence, the seed of the moral life.

I suggest then, by looking ever more subtly into one's own psyche so as to better observe humanity, by studying humanity in order to more truthfully comprehend oneself, by attempting to witness and thus become an artist of testimony, that the courage needed will be given by degrees. As Emerson said, "God will not have his work made manifest by cowards."

And as Rambert says in *The Plague*, "Until now I always felt a stranger in this town, and that I'd no concern with you people. But now that I've seen what I have seen, I know that I'm from here whether I want it or not. This business is everybody's business." And more recently, in the epigraph to her novel *Burger's Daughter*, Nadine Gordimer quotes Claude Lévi-Strauss: "I am the place in which something has occurred."

IV. Ethics: Toward an Open Wisdom

In his book *Fictional Structure and Ethics*, William J. Scheick suggests that the driving force of ethical narrative so prevalent in nineteenth-century literature was replaced, beginning at the turn of the century, with an almost exclusive interest in character. In novels by Émile Zola, Tolstoy, Dickens, George Eliot, and Dostoyevsky, characters exist to serve the ethical concerns of plot and to illustrate degrees of virtues and vice. The erosion of traditional Christian cosmology by the potent forces of Darwinism, imperialism, and industrialization was accompanied by a fascination with the shadowy psyche, with the theories of such scientists of the subterranean self as Sigmund Freud and the famous French hypnotist Jean-Martin Charcot. Conventional concepts of time and space, of cause and effect, were challenged by writers such as James Joyce and Virginia Woolf, in whose work the oedipal thrust of narrative was brilliantly overthrown for a more introspective and lyrically based narrative. The well-tempered plot, populated with obedient characters, gave way to the turbulent but thrillingly minute examination of slippery, complicated, intractable characters. The search for truth shifted ground; the symmetrical architecture of narrative began to yield to subjective ambiguity. Characters broke free of moralistic straitjackets; E. M. Forster claimed to have given up fiction because his characters refused to behave, wouldn't sit still for his well-planned portraits of them. The novel grew messier as its proportions and privileges shifted away from the classical ideal of the novel as aesthetic prescriptive, as aid to determining how best and most virtuously to live.

Somewhere in all of this, the ethically based narrative lost status, and is even today held in some slight contempt, regarded as a less honest form because it too overtly serves the author's bias, exiling itself from more admirable efforts at portraying an untidy, elusive reality. But all literature is rhetorical, all of us propagandists, with our implied author most urgently addressing our implied reader, even if only to say, Look, there is no meaning in any of this, you're as responsible as I am here, and neither of us is responsible at all, at least not in ways we can be certain of. The question then becomes how to be more fully aware of what it is we espouse. And it is my guess, though I have amassed no evidence, that in times of greater social upheaval and political repression, in times of collective human crisis, writers do respond, do redress the imbalance, do give passionate testimony. The novels of Harriet Beecher Stowe, Stephen Crane, Kate Chopin, John Steinbeck, Upton Sinclair, Harper Lee, Flannery O'Connor, Alexander Solzhenitsyn, Tim O'Brien, Don DeLillo, Toni Morrison, Nadine Gordimer, Alice Walker, J. M. Coetzee, Grace Paley, and Julia Alvarez, even when some of these authors' works might seem to sacrifice aesthetic proportion to the forces of moral outrage (if it was Virginia Woolf who cautioned against using fiction as a repository for one's rage, wasn't it Ernest Hemingway who believed the strongest writing emerged from a sense of injustice?)—I confess that even when some few of these works have beaten me about the head and shoulders with a kind of moral cudgel (I am thinking of Steinbeck's *Grapes of Wrath* and Alice Walker's

Possessing the Secret of Joy), why is it these books, marked by an overt concern with human values, with a sometimes ham-fisted questioning of good and evil, are still difficult to forget?

In advocating for greater engagement with ethical concerns in one's writing while losing none of the freedom achieved by breaking up the monopoly of male-centered nineteenth-century narrative, while losing none of our sophisticated focus on the interior world of characters, I would like to offer, in defense of my position, a clear distinction between two sorts of ethical systems. One I call open and morally engaged, the other closed and moralistic. The dangers of moralistic art are obvious: didacticism, dogmatism, shrill stridency of tone, not to mention a closing off of all avenues of truth save the one proclaimed. The dangers of moralistic thought are obvious as well, whether evinced in literature, politics, religion, or philosophical systems of thought, for here is a closed, fixed system of thought, demanding defense of that thought. Defense takes many forms, censorship, excommunication, exclusion, and misguided illusions of superiority and inferiority. There is a stasis to these closed forms of belief, an inertness resulting from a stagnant system with a limited power of authority and an overinvestment in premature closure. The most ominous temptation to any closed ethical system is that of judgment, of separation, of exclusion, of notions of superiority, all too frequently playing out in harmful acts of repression, censorship, violence.

Ralph Ellison said the understanding of art depends finally upon one's willingness to extend (open) one's humanity and one's knowledge of human life. In the open ethical stance, there is stillness of a different nature, not that of stasis or stagnation, but the stillness of waiting, of germination. In the open ethical stance, equality is presumed between reader and author, and the author stands accountable for what she says.

Both Thomas Merton and Simone Weil believed it essential

for the artist to remain free—not freedom as in license and a suspension of all values, but as a being so purely committed to the madness for truth, the genius for truth, that one's work is defined by openness, questing, questioning, a continual and perpetual flowering into compassion, and an empathic connection with all humanity. To be too tightly enclosed in any one dogma, creed, political system, or artistic theory may appear and feel initially safe, but as Beckett said in *Waiting for Godot*, "Habit is a great deadener." The artist might instead strive to be a wandering pilgrim, a mendicant, journeying from story to story, glimpsing the true, the sacred as it appears and manifests in each deceptively ordinary moment, as it transfigures the fictional landscape and its characters, before moving on.

When finally there are no fixed answers, only deeper and deeper questions, when tolerance is cultivated, the artist might come, in her writing, to more ideally reflect Spinoza's beautiful formula: "I have striven not to laugh at human actions, not to weep at them, nor to hate them, but to understand them."

As a student of Sufi teachings, Doris Lessing, in her preface to the French edition of *Seekers After Truth*, mentions the difference between Sufi parables that clearly give instruction in a particular issue and those subtler, more profound teaching stories that are enigmatic, that open outward, flowering into more questions, leading into finer and finer shades of knowledge and infinite degrees of truth. In the first sort of parable, the question is answered before the story begins; in the second, the story's question is posed so that to have no answer reveals the deepest kind of wisdom. So it is not dissident art I advocate for so much as moving beyond even that, into an awareness of the solitary act of writing as being a profound social act, the social act as being political, the political as being indistinguishable from the ethical, and the ethical as being inextricably linked to the spiritual. In short, we are none of us separate. As the Hopi say, our very breath connects us. Illusions of linear time, finite matter, the solitary self, the cordoning off of private from public, of religion from politics, of nation from nation, class from class, of ethics from art, all are illusions, albeit comforting, for they promise false security. And if illusions are, for all of us as human beings, sometimes necessary, as writers we must find the courage to move beyond these illusions of separation and exile to become architects of the vast, collective soul. We must eventually write, as Nadine Gordimer says, from the freedom of the grave.

Elephant in the Dark

*Some Indians kept an elephant in a dark room. Because
it was impossible to see the elephant, those who wanted to
know something about this exotic beast had to feel it with
their hands. The first person went into the darkness and
felt the elephant's trunk and announced, This creature is
like a water pipe. The next person felt the elephant's ear
and asserted, No. It's like a giant fan. A third person felt
the elephant's leg and declared, That's not true. This animal resembles a pillar. A fourth person felt the elephant's
back and concluded, Not at all. It's like a throne.*

*Different points of view produce different opinions. If
someone had brought in a candle, they would have all felt
like fools.*

—Sufi teaching story

A S A YOUNG, IMPRESSIONABLE WRITER, I once came across a
statement in a book on the craft of writing fiction declar-
ing point of view the most crucial choice any writer could make
at the outset of her story. Choosing the wrong vantage point
would doom a story to immediate failure. This gloomy bit of
news, offering no explanation, no reason for why this was so,
terrified me. Today, my beginner's terror has been replaced by
hard-won conviction. Now, I offer my own explanation, my

own reasons for believing point of view a pivotal, if not impera-
tive, authorial decision.

In the Sufi teaching tale offered above, each person believes
she can describe what an elephant is. The person touching the
leg metaphorically describes the leg, the person touching the
ear describes the ear, and so on. The whole body of the elephant
escapes each of the four individuals approaching it from four
different vantage points. That is the point of the teaching—each
person in the story, and by extension, each of us, is limited to
her own experience, her own vantage point and perception.
Were a candle or a lamp to be lit, each person would see her
own position, its humility, humor, and constraint. In light of
the vaster creature before her, she might then understand the
foolishness, or limit, of her own fixed opinion.

Understanding the restrictions of form, the fiction writer
can still consciously select her point of view in relation to a
wider view, some deeper meaning offered by the theme or ethical tension posited at the heart of her story. The most powerful
vantage point will suggest or infer the greater whole, cast light
on the body of the elephant in its dark room. If my character
stands here, she will see—and describe—mainly this. Standing
there, she will see—and describe—mainly that; each vantage
point reveals the nature of reality a little differently, and reality
reflects perception. Today, my own conviction about the
importance of point of view in fiction aligns with that of the
unremembered author's opinion of years ago. Point of view is
crucial to the success or failure of a story; the perspective the
writer selects must be the one that best illuminates her story's
deeper meaning and, by inextricable relation, uncovers a truth
or truths residing in her own heart.

Most often, when point of view is discussed as an element of
craft, the technical choice of first person ("I"), second ("you"),
or third ("he or she") is inevitably and necessarily raised. The

challenges of each choice are discussed—the positive effects of intimacy and authority rendered by use of first person versus the troubling danger of monotony and claustrophobic style. The unusual effect of second person, its way of putting emotional distance between a character and her truth. Then there are the "workhorse" capacities of third person, its less glamorous but dependably sturdy and occasionally profound range and effect. Such discussions of the technical effects of person are useful and important. During in-class writing exercises, my students are as impressed by the immediate authority of the "I" voice as they are eventually challenged by its boundaries. They enjoy experimenting with the unique slant offered by second person, and are gradually won over by the opportunities for character exploration offered by the third person. Writing exercises assigned both in and outside of class can be striking ways for students to practice the effects of first, second, or third person on a piece of fiction.

But point of view also has to do with who tells the story and from what vantage point in time, space, and memory. Many of my students begin by choosing the safest or most obvious character to tell the story, the character they feel they know best or can identify with most closely. Should a story about a father who is having a schizophrenic breakdown while driving his young daughter west across the desert be told from the point of view of the unraveling father, the innocent daughter, or the stranger they encounter? A recent student of mine struggled with this in her story, eventually choosing the point of view of the eight-year-old daughter who loves her father deeply and is only beginning to understand that while he may be quirky and adventurous, more so than most adults she knows, he shows increasingly poor judgment, putting her well-being in jeopardy, changing from the father she trusts to protect her, to a man who, under the spell of his own growing delusions, puts her into a danger from which she must extricate herself. Had this student told the story from the point of view of the father, it would have become his story, his journey, with the reader a witness to the father's tragic descent into mental illness. Had a stranger come along, becoming involved with a crisis in the lives of the father and daughter, we would have been introduced to that perspective, adding an additional layer, that of the stranger's life experience, and a character who then interprets the other characters' actions.

As a general rule, a story can have only one heart. Whose story is it? Which character owns the story most deeply? Ask these questions of your story, of your characters, at the outset. I often instruct students to visualize a great circle around the still fluid world of their imagined story, place their characters around the circumference of the circle, then move from one to the next, listening to each recount events from his or her point of view. Lend each character a candle to hold up to the body of the elephant, and see which casts the richest, most complex light, the most mysterious shadows. This act of imaginative listening proves remarkably accurate in unveiling the character who most truly owns the story, the one you will get the most emotional voltage out of, the most complex thematic and ethical currents.

Courage and patience are twin unheralded virtues of the fiction writer. Without realizing it, a writer might choose the most conservative path into a story both in terms of its action and its characters, limiting the story's power and arc of achievement. To sit patiently and wait to hear the story, internally, from each character's vantage point, sensing the emotional range in each voice, the glimpse of something greater offered beyond the character's narrow perspective, is one of the most useful "invisible" exercises to practice before setting the first sentence down on the page. Be inclusive of the most overlooked or least expected of your characters, for the humblest or least impressive figure may be the truest teller of the tale. Be open to surprise, to possibility, to the understanding that like your characters, you, too, are confined by specific experiences and perceptions. Be willing to expand perception, multiply experience. The author's magic is to find the point of view that casts the widest light into the darkness, that takes us on the furthest journey from the spot on which we ordinarily stand. In one recent student story, the author began with the viewpoint closest to her own, that of a young woman in college taking a summer job cleaning rooms at a swanky resort in Phoenix and describing her eccentric, disturbing friendship with another worker, an older man recently arrived from Eastern Europe. The story was well written in terms of language, style, and setting—her fellow students were impressed by the author's level of intelligence and sophistication. But something felt off. The story, while stylistically impressive, lacked power. In the best kind of collaborative classroom discussion, someone suggested the real heart of the story might lie with the older man from Eastern Europe. His air of emotional desperation, suggested by the author, had gone unexplored. Perhaps the most powerful story was his, not the young college girl's. The author took these suggestions to heart, and when she brought in her next draft for critique, the class was elated. She had given the story to the Eastern European, to a middle-aged man whose wife was terminally ill, a man half-mad from the wartime brutalization he had endured. By shifting the story from events and emotions belonging to a smart but fairly inexperienced college girl to this complex, suffering man, the story took on an emotional and ethical depth that was nothing short of stunning. By altering point of view, the student's new version cast the deepest shadow while yielding the greatest light. This is the undeniable power of point of view in fiction, its capacity to illumine the exterior world while laying bare the wilderness inside one human heart.

The Gift of Warwick

T HE TEN-WEEK TERM HAD ENDED, and we were enjoying a farewell party, something my writing students at Warwick University confessed they had never had before. The celebration was the result of a casual comment I had made one afternoon in class, to the effect that back in the United States, I nearly always hosted a party and book exchange in my home at the close of the semester. I wished I could do the same for my Warwick students, I had added, but living in a cramped room in London, two hours distant, made that unlikely. Within a day, class e-mails were exchanged, plans were fixed, and the party was on. Anna had generously offered her tiny dormitory kitchen and dining area, and now, thirteen of us were happily crowded around a table layered and messy with pans, plates of home-cooked food, and a dozen or more mostly empty bottles of wine. David Morley, the writing program director, stopped by for a visit and obligingly climbed on a chair to take group photographs. After he left, someone noted a red fox, resident of the nearby woods, slinking past the ground-level window, casting a sly, feral glance inside. How strange we must have looked to that fox, thirteen of us sitting quietly, listening with that singular, impassioned reverence students of writing give one another, as each took his or her turn around the table, reading from a newly revised story. Robin, Leila, Taylor, Anna, Zigian, Suzanne, Amy, Victoria, Nate, Sarah,

Laura, Mike. Emotions thickened the congenial atmosphere, feelings of affection, friendship, respect, the sharp poignancy of gratitude. Gratitude for the ten weeks shared, for bonds forged, for the hard, engaged work we had done, along with the shared, unspoken awareness that I would likely never see these students again. A flurry of jokes and contagious laughter failed to leaven the sudden, almost somber awareness of my departure the next day. There was an awkward silence. It's ended, I thought, my time with these students is over. I was adrift in this melancholy thought when Leila, with sweet formality, stepped up as the others sat strangely, conspiratorially, silent, to present me with a bouquet of flowers and a bag of wrapped and ribboned gifts, which when unwrapped, proved to be a book on travel, a teddy bear named Warwick, and a large, beautiful card they each had signed, a card I refused to open until I was alone in my hotel room. Their comments, as I knew they would, made me cry.

It had happened again, this time in a modest classroom at Warwick University, among a temporary community of thirteen British, Irish, and American writing students. We had created friendships based on a shared passion for fiction writing, an art calling for skillful observation, cultivated empathy, and emotional courage. As their teacher, I had served as catalyst, privileged witness to the emergence of a writing circle that strengthened and cheered on its members. Here was the true gift, that marvelous potential for a writing workshop to connect and transform lives, encouraging each writer to shine in honest, therefore eloquent, light.

What was I to do with the love I felt for each of these students? What had I given them that they had not returned tenfold? Three months later, I continue to receive occasional e-mails and letters. Everyone misses me, they say, sending news that one has won an award for a story worked on in class, another has an agent, a publisher interested in a novel worked on in class, another is newly married. They meet outside of the university schedule each week to read one another's work. Our circle, they tell me, endures.

Once, when Amy Tan was a visiting writer of the Piper Center for Creative Writing at Arizona State University, I spoke with her over dinner about teaching creative writing. She had never taught, she said. The concept made her terribly nervous, even worried—what if I hurt someone with my comments, what if I were to harm someone's writing process by saying the wrong or insensitive thing? Grateful for her acknowledgment of the gravity of a writing teacher's impact, I said I had those exact concerns every time I walked into a classroom on the first day of a new semester to meet a fresh group of students. I questioned my audacity, my easy assumption of such grave responsibility. Our conversation prompted me to think a bit more about what this kind of teaching was, exactly. Principles of craft were imparted, and the teacher's publishing experience and accomplishments lent credibility. But the highest measure of success in a creative writing workshop, I realized, had to do with the atmosphere engendered, the climate fostered, the careful cultivation of shared trust and safety, paired with an expectation of worthy effort and high standards. When the student-teacher dichotomy blurs, when we become a roomful of souls besotted with language, passionate in our shared belief in the transformative power of stories, when we take inspiration from one another's work, when we celebrate with food and wine, with gifts of books and readings from that work, when the single greatest story becomes the one we began shyly on the first day, with names and introductions, a story reaching its dramatic arc with goodbyes, a bittersweet moment followed by enduring connections of affection and support, then the writing workshop becomes a transcendent experience and, in my view, an unquantifi-able human success. Having formed a collective narrative, we become its creatures, its characters, giving ourselves traits of courage, affection, loyalty, and respect. Our circle goes on, a celebration, as ordinary yet rare as the fox, glimpsed and feral. Our story unfolds, elusive, vulnerable, fierce, replete with written, unwritten, still to be written beauty.

Doxology

Being a stretched-out hymn,
   a low hum of praise
to the Dachshund:

O! Whimsical, whizzical dash-hound!
To your perfectly droll, punctuational shape,
elastic comma, slimmest daschen of slinkdom—
short-legged, long-bodied little hunter!

Of thee I sing.

Being an Incomplete History of the Dachshund

MUMMIFIED DACHSHUNDS UNCOVERED in ancient Egyptian burial urns! It is false, this faint but persistent rumor of the Dachshund's Egyptian origin. Skeletal remains of low, stretched-out dogs suggestive of Dachshunds have been found in burial urns, and images of elongated dogs are etched on the tombs of two Egyptian kings, but no true, distinct link has ever been found. Peru, Mexico, Greece, and China have each been set forth as the Dachshund's point of origin, but sturdiest proof is found in sixteenth-century German woodcuts depicting a "low, crooked-legged little dog," unmistakably Dachshund shaped, tunneling for badgers, those ferocious, heavy-bodied omnivores of the weasel, or Mustelidae, family. Undisputed is the Dachshund's earth avocation, his primal reason for existence, to charge fearlessly into dark badger holes, or setts, to hold whatever unfortunate badger at bay as hunters dig down with shovels, guided by the Dachshund's muffled, tenacious bark—a grubby, perilous sport of human invention that the average house Dachshund would be mortified to ever imagine himself doing. These same house Dachshunds will be relieved to know that badger digging, occasionally accompanied by ladies with picnic baskets dining amusedly while their gentlemen friends dig and delve, was outlawed in Britain in 1973 and is illegal in a number of other European countries as well.

A common but distant ancestry is suspected between the ancient, French-bred Bassethound, *basset à jambes torses*, and the German-bred Dachshund, or *Teckel*. Both breeds possess overlong, tubular bodies, short legs with paddle-shaped paws, pendulous ears, and keen powers of scent. The Dachshund, however, has a proud spirit, an obstinate dignity absent in other hounds or in earth dogs like the terrier.

In 1839, as a marriage gift to the English queen Victoria, German prince Albert of Saxe-Coburg-Gotha presented his young wife with Waldmann, the first of her many beloved Dachshunds. A second Dachshund, Deckel, endeared himself to Victoria after he pounced on a rat in Windsor Castle: "The rat," said the queen, "made an awful noise, though he was killed right out rather quickly." One of the queen's troop of Dachshunds, Dacko, has been immortalized with a tiny bronze statue of himself poised somewhere on Windsor's grounds. Because of Victoria's fondness for Dachshunds, the Royal Collection includes a number of images of them in paintings and sketches. And since the queen's Dachshunds were observed in her royal company at all times, Victorian ladies, in a mad flattery of imitation, took to parading their own portable, close-to-the-ground and satchel-shaped Dachshunds through London's more elegant parks on sunny, mild afternoons. Embraced as a breed by British dog lovers, in the 1860s the first Dachshunds were formally shown as "German Badger Hounds" in classes for Foreign Dogs, and by 1873, separate shows for Dachshunds were held in the Crystal Palace exhibition halls. To satisfy the growing demand, a Mr. Schuller, remembered for no other reason, imported over two hundred Dachshunds from Germany in the winter of 1876.

With World War I, Dachshund popularity in Britain and America plummeted. Images of the Dachshund were used in war propaganda as symbols of the Teutonic empire. In Britain, feelings ran especially high against the Dachshund, and a documented report exists of one Dachshund being stoned to death on the high street of Berkhamsted. World War II stigmatized the breed a second time, and public knowledge that German Field Marshal Erwin Rommel, "The Desert Fox," kept Dachshunds as pets did not help—though must a Dachshund be held morally responsible for the notoriety of his or her owner? Lee Harvey Oswald's assassin, Jack Ruby, owned a dozen Dachshunds, one of whom, Sheba, he openly called his wife. Napoléon adored his Dachshunds, Grenouille and Faussette, while another, also named Napoléon, eased his disgrace on Elba.

Nomenclature

Formal

(der) Dachs (badger) *(der) Hund* (hound): of German origin
Dachs Kriecher (badger crawler)
Dachs Krieger (badger warrior)
Teckel
Dachel

Worshond
Dachsel
Dachchsen

Semi-Formal

Little burrow dog
Badger dog
Hole dog

Informal

Weiner
Sausage
Hot dog
Dash hound
Weenie
Doxie
Two dogs long

Foreign

Teckel or *Dashond* (Dutch)
Tax (Swedish)
Tacskó (Hungarian)
Jamnik (Polish)
Taksa (Russian)
Bassotto (Italian)
Basset d'Allemagne (French)

Soubriquets de S

Snoot
Snooter
Bug
Boy
Gunder

Schminker
L'il Si
Si-boy
Buddy
Shee-bo
Longfellow

Coats, Colors, Miniatures

> A dachshund is a half-dog high and a dog-and-a-half
> long.

> —H. L. Mencken

The Dachshund wears one of six coats of color: black and tan, chocolate and tan, cream, red, wheaten, and boar, and bears one of five sets of markings: dapple, piebald, double dapple, brindle, and plain. (The white Dachshund, a controversial breeding effort, remains an elusive, albinic ideal, a genetic Shangri-la.) The Dachshund's coat is smooth, longhaired, or wirehaired. A Smooth Dachshund, its shorthaired coat snugly encasing its muscular body much like an expensive Italian glove, is referred to simply as a "Smooth."

Dwarf *Teckels,* or Dwarf Dachshunds appeared in the nineteenth century, a German breeding effort. The tiny hounds, or *Kaninchenteckels,* were chiefly used as rabbit hunters. Displeased with the dogs' too-round skull, too-goggled eyes, and too-short ears, breeders persisted in efforts to produce a more perfect miniature of the standard size Dachshund. Success was achieved not in Germany but in Britain in the 1920s, when a "Miss F. E. Dixon, owner of the Kar Kennels of Smooths, exhibited a Smooth Miniature named 'Klein Kurio,' born in quarantine from German parents." Klein, a dwarf red, ignited a craze for diminutive *Teckels.* According to Mr. E. Fitch Daglish, many breeders and exhibitors of Standard Dachshunds "castigated the newcomers by describing them as toys, freaks and degenerates," but when the dwarves demonstrated they were as hardy and fearless and as strong in fieldwork as their larger relatives, criticism ceased. And when Colonel G. Spurrier, DSO, a widely respected name in Standard Smooths, stepped up to appoint himself President of the first Miniature Dachshund Club in 1935, the breed attained impervious respectability.

The Brief and Humble Lineage of S

Birthdate: November 29, 2004
Sire: Itty Bitty Inky
Dam: CC's Valentine
Gender: Male
Color: Black and Tan
Coat: Smooth
Size: Miniature

Daglish's Points

From *Standard of Points for the Miniature Dachshund* by Mr. E. Fitch Daglish, published by the Kennel Club, Great Britain, 1948:

> In conformation the Miniature Dachshund should be in all respects similar to the Dachshund of Standard size. It should be compact, short-legged and long in body, well muscled and strong, with bold and intelligent expression. The body should neither be so plump as to give an impression of cobbiness nor so slender as to impart a weasel-like appearance ... weight not exceeding 11 pounds ... any appearance of weediness or toyishness is to be avoided at all costs. The ideal weight is from 7 to 9 pounds.

To begin: S is a six-year-old dwarf Smooth, his coat a strict black with tobacco-colored trim on muzzle, paws, chest, or keel. His bottom is marked by a tobacco-brown "saddle," and above each of his round, black eyes, a polka dot of the same brown color lends keen expressiveness. S's nine-pound length is sinuous and elastic, something like the F-hole on a violin. On the rare occasion he worries, the otherwise glabrous space on his head between his ears rucks up in a neat corrugation like the tin roofing on a shed.

> The Miniature Dachshund should be gay, alert, bold and highly intelligent. Despite its small size it should be strong, extremely active, hardy and game. Movement should be free and gay.

This morning, out on the lawn, for instance, S lightly grips a small Frisbee between his teeth and prances, head high and proud, each paddle-shaped paw delicately lifting, before dropping the cloth disc at my feet, an invitation to play. I bend down, pick up his little orb, sail it through the mild, sunlit air. Giving chase, a tiny gazelle, he bounds, all four paws off the ground, before catching his prey in midair, seizing and shaking it, rat-a-tat-tat-tat, a rich, highly charged, drumming tattoo . . . "Oh, right, he's breaking its neck," one friend explained. Today's Frisbee equals yesteryear's badger. Inside the house, S snuffles and snorts swinishly in my bed, nosily rooting, tunneling, slinking, a dry otter beneath sheets and duvet, hunting down Frisbee, his surrogate mini-mammal, round and small and cloth, lime green, rimmed in neon pink. He has a basket of other toys, a squeaking hamburger, a beeping hot dog, a Walgreens limp raccoon and a Target puppet fox, both faux furred, factoried in China. S has licked the orange and black fox to stiff bits, dragging its honking, damp carcass about, a rank trophy stinking to high heaven. On occasion, I come upon it buried in my bed. But S's true portal to bliss is Frisbee, and in six years, I have replaced it dozens of times, since his incessant violent drumming of it on the ground inevitably results in a length of clear plastic tubing springing loose from its shredded cloth frame. Among his wide repertoire of Frisbee sports, the current indoor favorite calls for bed pillows to be heaped about on the bedroom carpet as I creep obligingly around, sliding a slow, teasing curve of Frisbee along the top edge of one of the pillows, until S runs and flings himself at it, the pillow smashing down, S tumbling over it, Frisbee escaping, whisked into another hiding crevice, perhaps beneath the pillow or inside its casing, as S careers madly about, scenting hard, panting, paws digging in comical, terrier-like frenzy, tail high and stiff, fast wagging, eyes bright, tracking down Frisbee—a fine domestic demonstration of the Miniature Dachshund's "free and gay" nature and of his medieval beginnings as a hunter of badgers.

Amphibian

After S has fetched my swimsuit from the floor of the closet and dropped it at my feet, no longer patient with my dawdling and poking about, I am at last where he has wanted me since he woke at dawn: upright in the swimming pool's shallow end. He stands beside me on the pool's curved edge, Frisbee between teeth, tail a conductor's slim, black baton, blurring with metronomic energy, before he deftly releases the cloth disk into the water, watching with fixed, obsessive delight as I snatch it up and after a bit of sly feinting and dodging, making him guess where it will go, to the left or to the right, high or low, fling it above the grass. As the disk skims, off he goes, a lithe, swift slink, chasing, seizing, drumming, tearing back, dashing along the lip of the pool to drop it again, often with a flip of deliberate grace, into the water. Seamless orb catcher, trick dog, circus dog, do I imagine a tulle ruff of red and white polka dots around your arched neck? One . . . two . . . three . . . drawing highest suspense out of the moment, I pitch the Frisbee high and straight this time. S races, gazing skyward, nine out of ten times catching it perfectly, drumming it (one marvels he doesn't sprain his neck, that same friend said), running a victory dash with it before returning to the pool's shallow end to once again drop his prey into the water and gaze at me with tireless, blissful expectancy. Play! These summer morning pool games proceed with relentless vigor. I try to sneak in a few exercise laps as S trots poolside, stalking me, sometimes dropping the Frisbee into the deep end, a variation on his own rules. For the past two summers he has not wanted to get into the water, something he once loved to do. I miss S's sedate glide into the water from the steps, paddling about in joyful circles, or the way he would launch himself with airborne aplomb from the side of the pool. I miss how he would climb onto my legs as I swam the breaststroke, trot gaily up their length until reaching the pale island of my back where he would plant himself, front paws on the back of my head, gazing fixedly ahead, charting the horizon, a solemn figurehead poised atop his mistress as she chugged through cool, aquamarine waters.

Something must have spooked him, for S swims only occasionally now, and with sad, fearful caution. These days he seems happiest standing on the top pool step, letting water lap around his belly before getting out and shaking himself with that flapping, loose skin shuffle, whappity-whap, before taking to a slope on the lawn, tumbling over onto his back in the sunwarmed grass, writhing and audibly groaning with pleasure, before springing contentedly to his feet, sprinkled with a confetti of grass bits.

Baguette

Little compares with the sensation of S, burrowed beneath the blankets and top sheeting of the bed, stretched at full, luxuriant length alongside my thigh or back, tiny paws kneading my skin in dream, a warm, breathing baguette, a snortling, tubular hot water bottle. Pleasant, until I realize he is dead center in the bed, in its softest part, while I perch precariously, a hairless herring or naked eel, on the lip of the mattress, a flesh outcropping beginning to ache. In sleep, I had courteously relinquished my space to him, and now his long, toasty bolster body is aligned along my leg. Upon waking, he swims, crocodile-ish, up from the bed's warm depths to bestow kisses with his pink tongue and cold slimy snout on my glued-shut eyes and weakly protesting mouth.

Set no alarm, Mistress of S, own no timepiece, for the Baguette slithers forth from his drowsy underworld at the same hour, each and every day of the week—at 6:00 a.m.

Xylophone

The Dachshund's peculiar shape has inspired commentary from cartoon sketches and children's books to humorous imitation, from kitschy salt and pepper shakers to bookends, ashtrays, and the like. His shape lends itself to easy metaphor—pretzel, noodle, loaf, baguette, wiener, sausage, low bench, and just yesterday, as I petted him, running my hand down his blue-black length, this long-spined creature with four legs when six might prove a better engineering solution—he suddenly became a tuneless xylophone. A xylophone! As a child, I was once given a toy xylophone, each metal key painted a different bright hue, the thing meant to be struck with a stick that had a wooden knob at one end. I was supposed to bang along the length of the metal keys according to instructions provided by a booklet of simple songs, their tunes marked out to match the colors and numbers painted on each key. "Mary Had a Little Lamb" might be two red, two red, three yellow, two red, four blue, four blue, four blue, etc. I was entranced and insulted by this metal instrument, one that could be dragged along the floor, like a pet, by a yellow plastic leash. Insulted by its simplistic design and stupid songs, yet entranced because armed with a booklet of stupid songs and a knobbed, wooden stick, I could bang out an inane but recognizable tune. I remembered all this as I massaged S's spine, the Dachshund's Achilles heel, as he groaned mightily from some Jonah-depth of belly. If you were a xylophone, dear S, I would play you gently, tap a silent tune along your long, long, long spine: one black, two tan, one black, two tan, two tan, three pink, three pink, three pink. "How Much Is That Doggie in the Window?" Of course he would not stand still for such nonsense.

Matador

Obsessively loyal, S waits to hear the crunch of the car wheels on the graveled driveway, the tootling of the horn that announces I'm back from wherever it was I dared go without him. A sentry, he stands at the double front doors, glass trimmed in a white wood frame, his motionless head rising only a few inches above the bottom frame, tiny, triangular, black, and shaped like a matador's hat, a *montera*. His eyes fix on my approach, his tail held in straight salute, still as a reed; he refuses to wag it until he hears the sound and certainty of my key turning in the lock.

May Queen

S's ears are slim, shaped rather like tongue depressors. Velvety black on their outsides, at the lower underside of each tender, pendulant ear the black fades to grayish pink, then further up, where the skin turns bare, increasingly pinked, rosy, the flap leads up into the ear canal itself. When he plays, both ears sometimes fly back and stay cocked backward, exposing the pink, complex, shell-like entrance to the ear. With this, S acquires a delicate, feminine look, as if he is wearing a coronet, a garland, a diadem of pink cockleshells or tiny, ballet-pink rosebuds. Other times, a single ear flap cocks back, revealing the rosy whorls and swirls of that ear, while the other still hangs down, a soft, black, ovate leaf, giving him a jaunty, debonair, Parisian look.

Harbor Seal

During much of my California childhood, my grandparents lived a few blocks from the Sacramento Zoo. Every summer morning during the two weeks I stayed with them, I woke to the loud, ragged roaring of lions eager for their raw breakfast meat. It was like waking to Africa. Whenever my father took me to the zoo (and as I recall, he was the only one who did), I made a beeline not for the lions but for the brown mottled harbor seals in their rock-hedged pool. If we were lucky, we arrived in time to watch as one of the zoo workers, in a white uniform, put his hands into the briny waters of a white plastic bucket and brought out a silver, glittering mess of fish, tossing them in a wet, gleaming arc like newly minted coins toward the cluster of seals, who barked and curved their necks back to catch the fish in their mouths. I was quite mad about these seals, their wet, sleek, curved forms, their enormous, lustrous eyes, their smooth, water-polished heads. Gripping the chain-link fence, in unselfconscious eight-year-old mimicry, I barked right along with them. My wise father never shushed or discouraged me, never acted as if his tomboy daughter's intense longing to be a seal, her wild, hoarse barking, was anything other than normal.

S, when swimming, sleek head raised above the water, feet

paddling beneath, is a tiny version of those zoo seals I loved as a child. He barks as they did, though not in chorus and not for fish, but to guard and to protect me, or in a half-rapturous, half-impatient appeal to play.

Barbell

Self-explanatory. He is shaped much like a tiny hand weight with feet, his triangular, long and slim-nosed head reminiscent of an alligator's, or a pair of needle-nose pliers, or the Geico car insurance lizard.

> In the home the Teckel is a lover of comfort and very ready to accept the role of the sleek, pampered voluptuary. But a life of cushioned ease is not good for him. His right place is in the open fields and woods, where his keen senses and lithe, sinewy body may be put to the use for which they were evolved. A soft, fat Dachshund is never happy.

S Motoring

Observe dear S, back feet tiny as a squirrel's, balanced vertically on my thigh, front feet on the car's window ledge, gazing solemnly out at the passing world, long ears blowing like curtains in the breeze, sunlight tingeing his short black coat with glints of soap-bubble iridescence. His expression is grave, intent, focused, as if this motoring is reverent business. Two blocks before approaching the intersection where I would turn if we are going to the veterinarian, which usually we are not, S flows, an inky slinky, off my lap, disappearing under the passenger's seat. Even if he is still there, hiding beneath the seat, he knows as I turn into our driveway that we are home. Should I turn down a particular street, he knows we are near my daughter's home and starts lunging to get out of the car.

How does he see, scent, remember, know? I try to fathom his Dachshund's intelligence through my human one.

The Soft, Fat Dachshund Who Loathed His Walk

Like all voluptuaries, S assumes a degree of winter indolence that, even in mild Arizona, is impressive. His long sleeps are hibernatory. As a consequence, he inflates, grows bloatish and stout. Since my house is on a busy road, behind a wall and not conducive to dog walking, this winter, I seize upon the notion of driving S to my daughter's house twice a week to go on walks. In tandem, we will teach S to do what normal dogs do, perambulate down sidewalks. This, I reason, will slim S down and be a salutary change of pace for him.

On the first day, the three of us, S on an unaccustomed leash, head out into the quiet street, an old-fashioned university neighborhood full of quaint houses, large yards, and people walking dogs. After only a few steps, still in the driveway, S begins to slither close to the ground, balking, then stopping, a tiny mule with bared teeth. Somehow, we persuade him to proceed, but he loathes every step, snarls at a jogger passing by, cowers while speeding past a tied-up, baying Basset Hound (his relative!), S, a weasel wiener, soft belly grazing the sidewalk, strains against his leash at a curbed, slow-motion gallop toward home. He doesn't seem to realize he is to take leisurely pleasure in first scenting, then peeing on whatever takes his fancy. He merely tries to drag us, in straight-arrow, eel-like fashion, down the street and back into my daughter's home, where, upon arrival, he will lap up an entire dish of water before burrowing under a soft throw blanket and plunging straight back into hibernation. Weeks pass this way before S begins to relax a little. Going down the sidewalk a little distance one day, he lifts his leg against a forlorn shrub, finds that same woeful shrub, ever more forlorn, the next day, and with an air of dignity and familiarity—oh, you, dear growth!—sprinkles it again. We are careful to proceed along the same route each time until recognition and pattern take hold, until some slight shift in S's brain tells him that perhaps this is not an utter nightmare. Today, he still does not relish his walks, yet neither does he resist them. He marches stolidly, if grimly, along, lifts his leg diplomatically on his old markers, finds new ones, is unfazed by joggers and part of the dog-walking world now. And while I cannot claim this as a direct consequence, S has recently begun to emerge from the car to accompany me on errands. He trots on his leash into the dry cleaner's, the mailing service, the hardware store, still deeply cautious, tail belted tight under his bottom, but nonetheless assuming a role in the greater world of travel and commerce. When I consider his bit of long body set down into the enormity of the world, its noise and clamor and dangers, I find S's new, excursionary derring-do a very brave achievement. And as a result, he has trimmed down, is neither cobby nor weaseled, toyish nor weedy.

S's Masseuse

Twice a month I receive massages at home from my friend Clara, a Native American masseuse and healer. Before my massage, we enjoy tea and conversation, and in the winter, as it is now, the massage table is set up in the living room, near the fireplace.

With the fire neatly blazing and a track of soporific spa music playing, I settle in, stomach down, under blankets on the table, cradle my head in the round massage cushion with its open hole in which to put my face. As I gaze down at the carpet, S dances on his hind legs to kiss and lick my pinioned face before contentedly settling into a chair to doze in the firelight and await his turn. S worships Clara with melting adoration, and though she and I can't remember exactly when or why this began, my massage is invariably followed these days by S's.

He watches intently, Clara reports, while she works on me. As if waiting. When my session is over, he stands beside the table until I lift him up to its surface, then lies down cooperatively. Perched on one side of the table, Clara begins to lightly rub S, to stroke him, paying special attention to his long spine, shoulders, and hips. A willing sybarite, he shifts from long side to long side, goes limp, groans with pleasure, his eyes worshipful on his masseuse, occasionally raising his head a little to tenderly kiss her hand. "He is like a little man," Clara says. "I always see him wearing a top hat with a cane." S is now as much a client of Clara's as I am. When his session, by his own indication, ends, after about twenty minutes, he is gently lowered to his realm of floor where he races in frenzied loops and blurring circles, unable to contain his exuberance, finds his Frisbee, tears back and drops it on Clara's feet as thanks. After she leaves, I will find him in bed, on his back, all four paws aloft, basking in the afterglow of his spa treatment.

Church of Repetition

For S, routine is a holy world order; his daily habits sacrosanct. For example:

3:30 a.m.	Nightly wee in the yard
6:00 a.m.	Rise and shine, Frisbee in beak
6:05 a.m.	Dish of Cesar
6:10 a.m.	Outside to relieve himself
6:15 a.m.	Back in bed, under the covers, for a long snoot snooze
9:00 a.m.	Up with his mistress for a smackerel of her breakfast

From the Handwritten Pet Sitter's Guide to S:

> Important! He has developed an odd aversion to his
> doggy door. He will try to get you to let him into the
> house through regular doors. Don't. Firmly persuade him
> to come in through his own little door. (One day, I found
> him outside the laundry room door, nearly perished of
> heatstroke, because he refused to come inside through
> the doggy door . . . so please keep an eye on him.)
>
> Monsoon Season and Rain! He refuses to pee in the
> rain, so I have to put his leash on and take him out the
> front door to three little shrubs on the immediate right,
> beneath the roof overhang, it stays dry there, and he will
> hustle out and pee and then shoot straight back inside.

S Parlance

If language is a window into culture, here is a plate-glass gaze
into S's world, his lingual society, the words and phrases he
recognizes and responds to: cheese, hamburger, chickee strip,
popcorn, ice cream, Cesar (the name of his previous wet food,
now Newman's Own gourmet organic turkey and chicken formula—when I got a raise, he did, too), Frisbee, toy, foxy (the
stinky thing that honks at both ends), outside, swim swim,
swimsuit, go for a ride, car, go for a walk, leash, give me a kiss,
good boy, what a good boy, little boy, sit (he will), stay (he
won't), S, S-boy (additional soubriquets listed above), no, go
outside, go poddy, pee pee on the grass, go poddy outside, play,
drop it, Caty (my daughter), Clara (see Masseuse), catch, one
two three . . . up the ramp, go up the ramp (see Bedside Ramp).

S is deathly afraid of foreign languages. When I practice
my Italian aloud, he scuttles under the bed and hides until I
start making sense again. And while S knows close to fifty English words and phrases, a few gain seasonal prominence. His

summer favorites are "swim swim" and "swimsuit." S has been known to fetch my swimsuit from the closet floor and drop it at my feet, indicating his impatience with my slothful practice of sitting in bed with my laptop all morning. He, of course, needs no suit; his sartorial requirements as a Smooth never extend beyond his neat little mitten of black hair with tobacco trim. When he sits and watches me dress, I imagine him puzzling over why I have to "change skins" so frequently. And when I sit at my desk in my study too long, sighing, in front of the lit screen of my laptop, printing and stuffing papers in the trash can, he lays nearby on his sheepskin, watching, and, I am certain, pitying me. Why won't I pay heed? Eat, play, love, with a fourth action—nap. This is the formula for bliss. And in S's world, play is active prayer.

Daglish's Faults

Here our Mr. Daglish, in his famous *Standard of Points*, states the miniature Dachshund's "major faults":

> Round skull. Round or protruding eyes. Short ears. Shallow chest. Narrowness in front or behind. Short body. Long legs. Splayed feet. Cow hocks. Undershot or overshot mouth. Nervous or cringing behavior. Wooly or curly coat.

I don't see any of the above on S, though he is possessed of a seventh nipple. Pinkish gray and wart-like, it rides aslant over the front left-hand nipple. He also has a slight crease in one ear, and a propensity, during times of stress (his mistress traveling far and too long from him), to go bald around the chest, keel, and the backs of his ears. After she returns, his hair does, too.

While S's primary colors are black and tan, these are ornamented by the inside shell pink of his ears, the deeper rose of his tongue, and the hot, fiery pink of his tiny shoot of penis, which missiles out whenever lady friends come to visit, embarrassing, even paining him with its uncontrollable, fiery glisten of tension. Not a fault, I imagine Daglish saying, only nature.

Pale Writ in Urine

> The Teckel is by nature self-willed and has a strong sense of his own importance, but he is sensitive to correction, anxious to please and very appreciative of praise. All instruction should be given with due regard to the pupil's mentality.

Not noted in any of Mr. Daglish's precise writings on miniature Dachshunds is the anatomical "fault" of a leaky, or perhaps sneaky, bladder. Dwarf Dachshunds are notoriously difficult to housebreak—for one thing, they are independent, intelligent, pleasure oriented, and find it easy to outwit their owners. While peeing outside in clement weather is one of S's pleasurable rituals (and to see a tiny, nine-pound noodle delicately hoist his rear leg against the base of a sixty-foot palm tree and stream forth with enormous dignity and aplomb is unforgettable), why pee outside, in the glary sun, bothersome wind, nasty rain, or demonically cold snow, why micturate in rough elements, when it's ever so much nicer and makes everything smell so pleasantly familiar to whiz inside? (I am trying to penetrate the mind and motives of S . . .)

S's propensity to indoor watering displeases his mistress, so ever thoughtful, he wees when she's not looking. I have never once come upon S in the act. I have no idea when he does this as he seems to always be fastened, a long, adoring limpet, to my side, and one glance of displeasure after the fact or a single sharp word of reprimand is met with a quick scuttle under the bed. Out of sight, etc.

There is some droll, deliberate artistry to all of this. A green velvet chaise longue in the sitting area of my bedroom was once targeted by a precisely measured pattern of polka dots around its otherwise elegant form. When I purchased a pair of ficus trees in clay pots and placed them in the flagstone foyer, they became fresh targets for his covert urinary adventures. I purchased a good-looking, costly wooden dog gate to keep him out of the carpeted living room, but one unanticipated consequence is I don't go in there anymore either, except when guests visit and I have to remove the gate. The doors to the carpeted guest bedroom and bath are always kept closed. As I write this, it occurs to me that one third of my house is effectively sealed off from both of us.

Another quirk of his faulty or sneaky bladder, especially humiliating to poor S, is the way his penis responds to those visitors he is delighted to see. In his excitement to greet them at the door, pee shoots forth like a garden sprinkler from his scarlet pizzler, eliciting amusement, a horrible embarrassment to S. He tries everything to subdue said pizzler, sitting on it, hunching over it, placing his tongue on its end like a stopper. As he's aged, this social anguishment has abated slightly, but what has barely slowed is his priestly christening of my house—the twin potted ficus trees and a spot of flagstone by the front door remain favorites. After trying everything humanely conceivable to correct S's covert pizzling and wizzling, I now accept this as his major, his chief, his uncorrectable fault. He may not be possessed of a round skull or protruding eyes, cow hocks or an overshot mouth, flaws our Mr. Daglish finds objectionable, but his bladder, perhaps the size of a concord grape and as miniature as the rest of him, is in constant communication with the world. Perhaps because I am a writer, he imitates, scribbling his own minute, foreign communiqués. Perhaps his tiny liquid expressions are a rebel art form, like graffiti. And after the act, if not in hiding, he will solemnly study, read with his long nose, the runes of his pee.

An Ardor for Females

> Anyone who sets out to train a Dachshund must first win its confidence and co-operation. Nothing is more obdurate than an obstinate Dachshund.
>
> ... Miniature varieties may be kept without inconvenience, even in small flats. He is alert, fearless, affectionate and hardy, so that he makes an admirable guard; while his high intelligence, loyalty, unfailing sense of humor and adaptability endear him to all who have the good fortune to know him intimately.

All women are goddesses, evoking S's sycophantic adoration. Men, by contrast, are large, loud, noxious fixers to be barked off, snarled at, and, if necessary, ankle nipped. S would have a harem of women around him if he could, and he does have a man or two he deigns to like, but when professional men arrive to repair something around the house or yard, or to deliver pizza or packages, he is unrepentantly aggressive. Most of these men laugh good-naturedly at the sight of a long, small dog possessed of such ferocious attitude and furious noise, but in the event he darts forward to take precise aim at their ankles, it becomes another story. I have taken to coaching all visitors, before arrival, to gaze up at the ceiling as they enter the foyer— never look down, I warn, and by all means, never bend down and say "Hi there, little fellow," such condescension guarantees a nip. Ignore S. Act as if he does not exist. This gives him leeway to creep over, sniff your shoes, determine origins and motives. Absurd, but there it is. I am no dog whisperer. If S has faults, I do, too. If I haven't followed proper dog-schooling procedures, his faults, ergo, stem from mine.

> Dachshunds usually have good appetites. They tend to be
> greedy rather than fastidious in the matter of food.

From one thousand feet away, S can hear the refrigerator door open, identify the sound of a package of cheddar cheese opening, can distinguish between that and the lid coming off of an ice cream carton. He turns up his long, slender snout at microwaved, artificially seasoned popcorn, and only eats home-popped popcorn if it is buttered. His manner of begging, elegant, minimalistic, is to sit at your feet and stare unblinkingly until you relent and slip him a tidbit. Visitors at the dining table remark on his irresistible methods, and if a chair is vacant he somehow quietly appears on it. If no one is looking, he will be up on the table itself in seconds, and if no one objected, would stroll from plate to plate to sample what is rightly his. (This latter has never happened.) Our friends fall into categories: those who are cool toward animals and thus impervious to S's charms, those who think he is uncannily human and adorable, those who are disgusted by a Miniature Dachshund wandering about the surface of a dining room table, and those who laugh merrily as I pick him up and restore him to the floor. You can imagine who we are happiest to have visit us. In past years, long before S, I sometimes invited my pet hens, Doris and Betty, a Rhode Island Red and a Plymouth Rock, into the kitchen, where they sat on my lap and pecked off my plate. I once coaxed my daughters' pet Appaloosa, Pal, into a rented kitchen in the countryside to drink from the sink spigot as he stared curiously through the window at the pasture he had just wandered in from. And I once bought a spring lamb and let him dash through the house a while, entertaining my children, until I tethered him outside in the yard. Like animal crackers in soup, animals in houses are fun. So a miniature Smooth perched politely on a chair or padding daintily across the dining room table is neither alarming nor offensive to me, but a part of my libertine, slightly wacky philosophy of animal egalitarianism.

Bedside Ramp

> *The Dachshund's affectionate,*
> *He wants to wed with you:*
> *Lie down to sleep,*
> *And he's in bed with you.*
> *Sit in a chair,*
> *He's there.*
> *Depart,*
> *You break his heart.*

—E. B. White

Because of their tubular, Giacometti shape, Dachshunds are prone to severe spinal injuries. The owner of a Dachshund is cautioned never to let his pet jump off high places or use stairs. Like much nineteenth-century German royalty, I was allowed only Dachshunds as pets while growing up, and one of our family's Dachshunds, a black Smooth named George, did become paralyzed and had to be euthanized, a memory that haunts me, accompanied by guilt over my childish and ignorant cruelties to him, dressing him up in dolls' clothes, forcing him inside an upside-down straw wastebasket so I could watch him spin around and around trying to get free, something I thought hilarious. So S, after a mild injury to his spine when he was a puppy, now has a carpeted, custom ramp to run up and down alongside my bed. As a single woman, I have endured a fair amount of jokes about this ramp, and that is all I will say on the subject.

One day I came into my bedroom and found S lying under the covers, on his back, head on my pillow, front paws tucked neatly over the edge of the folded sheet. He looked at me, following me with his gaze as I moved through the room. It was unsettling. I walked over and looked down at him. Who are you, I asked. My husband? Wisely, he did not answer.

Following that unanswered question, I conceived of writing an arch, clever tale of a Dachshund who like, Kafka's cockroach, but in a reversed, more gradual process, turns into a woman's fourth husband. I began the story but abandoned it when I awoke one morning to find S lying straight alongside me, head perfectly aligned with mine. When I turned to look at him, he stretched out his neck to give me a peck, which smelled of gaseous fermented kibble. It was as if my tale had come true, and my common-law spouse was unemployed, eons younger than me, and of Germanic (not ancient Egyptian) extraction. He was not a tall, dark, handsome prince under a spell but S, loaf shaped, stubby legged, beef breathed, and neutered.

The Doxologist's Long Hymn and Low Hum of Praise

One of my self-imposed conditions or caveats in attempting to write about S was to not wax sentimental, to not turn saccharine or mushy over how irreplaceable, how precious and adorable, how unutterably perfect he is—so I hit upon the notion of a brief history of Dachshunds, celebrity facts, breeding standards, etc., all while working my way toward S—but now I think: why be coy about passion for one's dog? Why dissemble? Why hide such love? Those who love dogs will understand perfectly, those who don't probably aren't reading this anyway. Praise away, then! Let your words meet your title: Doxology.

In his little earthly span, S has freely given cheer, consolation, and solace not only to me but to nearly everyone he meets. During the long, awful months my mother was slowly failing from a stroke, I would take S on a near daily basis to visit her. Toward the end, the only time she laughed outright was when he raced in to see her, leaping like a long, slim gazelle onto her bleak hospital bed, rushing up to kiss her face and to snuggle beside her. When I pushed her wheelchair through the care center's garden, he gaily trotted alongside us. Sitting at the outdoor table, she shared what food she could still eat with him, while S gave my mother the last bits of joy in her life.

When I have been brokenhearted by disappointment or betrayal or loss, S will find me, smother me, wriggle all over, slather me with kisses. If I incur a minor wound, a tiny injury, he sniffs it out, nuzzles it in sympathy.

This tenderness cannot be overestimated, nor the depth of his affection minimized.

When I return from a long trip, S waits for me to set my suitcase down on the bedroom floor, to unzip it so he can dive deep into its contents, root around, sniffing, tracing all the places I have been.

What impresses me most, since I am a writer given to solitary contemplation tinged with melancholy—is S's consistent, undiminished happiness, his unwavering adoration and good humor—no matter how I appear, no matter where on the scale of off putting or enticing I might fall on a given day, there is no partial or conditional affection from S.

His love and loyalty are absolute.

Be the person your dog thinks you are, I read somewhere. Well, I do try to be that person, a reflection of him, actually, cheerful, loving, ready to play or to luxuriate in a nap or a good snack, to be a loyal voluptuary, a Smooth, guarding all that is precious and dear.

Six years ago my younger daughter and I brought S home, a six-week-old puppy. Still unnamed, he fit inside the palm of my hand, an enlarged comma, a velvety soft punctuation mark. Today, middle aged, fighting portliness and a fondness for rich foods and lassitude (not unlike his mistress), he weighs an average human newborn weight of eight pounds.

He has a thin rime of silver beard under his chin, and sometimes he limps after playing hard, a foreshadowing of the one inevitability I cannot bear to think about. S is not some Kafkaesque husband, but he is a merry sidekick, a boon companion, a confederate in pleasures both simple and subtle, the finer, altogether nobler, half of me.

> Eat, Play, Love, Nap
> Little shadow. Elongation of light.
> Simon

ADDENDUM: DACHSHUND TRIVIA

Celebrity Dachshunds

French impressionist Pierre Bonnard retained Dachshunds as companions. One of them may be seen in the foreground of *Nude in the Bath and Small Dog* (1946).

Pablo Picasso's Dachshund, Lump ("loomp," German for "rascal"), slept with him, dined from his master's own dishes, and found himself, as in the case of the famous black rendering of *Lump* on a white dinner plate, the subject of Picasso's art. "Lump," said Picasso, "he's not a dog, he's not a man, he's someone else." The book *Picasso and Lump: A Dachshund's Odyssey* was written by Picasso's friend, photographer David Douglas Duncan. Lump died after Picasso, but in the same year, 1973.

Andy Warhol traveled about with his pair of Dachshunds, Amos and Archie, whom he frequently painted and wrote about in his diaries.

David Hockney described his pair of Dachshunds, Stanley and Boodgie, subjects of his portraits in *Dog Days*, as "intelligent, loving, comical, and often bored."

British author P. G. Wodehouse probably modeled his most popular character, Jeeves, after his Dachshund, Bertie. "It is fatal to let any dog know that he is funny, for he immediately loses his head and starts hamming it up." Like Picasso's Lump, Bertie died shortly after Wodehouse.

From Mark Twain's travelogue *Following the Equator*:

> In the train, during a part of the return journey from Baroda, we had the company of a gentleman who had with him a remarkable looking dog. I had not seen one of its kind before, as far as I could remember, though of course I might have seen one and not noticed it, for I am not acquainted with dogs, but only with cats. The dog's coat was smooth and shiny and black, and I think it had tan trimmings around the edges of the dog, and perhaps underneath. It was a long, low dog, with very short, strange legs—legs that curved inboard, something like parentheses turned the wrong way. Indeed, it was made on the plan of a bench for length and lowness. It seemed to be satisfied, but I thought the plan poor, and structurally weak, on account of the distance between the forward supports and those abaft. With age the dog's back was likely to sag; and it seemed to me that it would have been a stronger and more practicable dog if it had had some more legs. It had not begun to sag yet, but the shape of the legs showed that the undue weight imposed upon them was beginning to tell. It had a long nose, and floppy ears that hung down, and a resigned expression of countenance. I did not like to ask what kind of a dog it was, or how it came to be deformed, for it was plain that the gentleman was very fond of it, and ... I could see that he was proud of it, not-withstanding it was such a long dog and looked so resigned and pious.

Henry James kept a pet Dachshund named Max, Dorothy Parker had Robinson, and James Joyce, J. D. Salinger, and William Faulkner were all owned by Dachshunds.

E. B. White on his trio, Fred, August, and Minnie:

> Being the owner of dachshunds, to me a book on dog discipline becomes a volume of inspired humor. Every sentence is a riot. Some day, if I ever get a chance, I shall write a book, or warning, on the character and temperament of the dachshund and why he can't be trained and shouldn't be. I would rather train a striped zebra to balance an Indian club than induce a dachshund to heed my slightest command . . .
>
> When I address Fred I never have to raise either my voice or my hopes. He even disobeys me when I instruct him in something he wants to do.

German Kaiser Wilhelm II kept a pack of Dachshunds, among them, Wadl, Hexl, Senta, and Erdmann. Wadl and Hexl, a ferocious duo, nearly ignited an international incident after they did away with one of Archduke Franz Ferdinand's prized golden pheasants while visiting the Austro-Hungarian's estate, Château Konopiště

In early *Mickey Mouse* comic strips, Mickey's sidekick was a Dachshund, Weenie.

A partial list of Hollywood star and celebrity Dachshunds include Marlon Brando's Oscar, Clark Gable and Carole Lombard's Commissioner, Rita Hayworth's Knockwurst, Doris Day's Ruby and Schatzie, James Dean's Strudel, and Cindy Crawford's Gerbil. Errol Flynn, John Wayne, Gloria Swanson, Joan Crawford, Vincent Price, Elizabeth Taylor, Katharine Hepburn, Madonna, and Heidi Klum have all owned, or been possessed by, Dachshunds.

Dachshund Foolery

The Wiener Nationals take place in California, Texas, Arizona, Kansas, Oklahoma, Minnesota, and Ohio. Pittsburgh hosts an annual Wiener 100, and Huntington, West Virginia, sponsors an annual Dachshund Dash.

Dachshund festivals are held in the Mid-Atlantic and the Midwest. On the last Saturday in April, a Dachshund Spring Fiesta, complete with an anthem, "The Dachs Song," is held in Washington Square Park, New York.

The Dachs Song

There's no other dog like a Dachshund
Walking so close to the ground,
They're stubborn and sly as a fox and
The happiest pet to be found.

Most kinds of dogs seem to either
Have shapes or proportions all wrong,
They're only one way or the other,
But Dachshunds are both short and long.

Dachsie, meine dachsie,
The best canine under the sun,
Call you "wiener" or "sausage" or "hotdog,"
We know that you're number one.

—composed by Murray Weinstock and Paul de Vries

Wiener Takes All, a dogumentary by Shane McDougall, has this theme song:

So sleek, so strong, so short, so long
With the grace of a gazelle, you run.

So sweet, so Odd—So perfectly flawed
In this doggie world you're number one!

CHORUS
Wiener Takes All
As you fly inches high from the ground
Keep your eyes on the prize
Even if you should stumble or fall
Weiner Takes All

Big ears, small feet, will work for treats
Doxie you've got Moxie in your stride

A flash, a blur—that face, that fur
Your style and grace can never be denied . . .

CHORUS (etc.)

And finally, in the town of Zelenogorsk, Russia, a parade of Dachshunds passes by a Dachshund monument every July 25, "City Day," while in Gergweis, Germany, the "Dachshund Capital of the World," there are two Dachshunds for every Gergweisian, and a tourist can rent a Dachshund as a walking companion.

A Solemn Pleasure

Helen Reilly Brown
July 14, 1918–April 6, 2008

Clarence John "Jack" Brown, Jr.
April 17, 1918–June 13, 2003

Cremation Requirements

Cremation is performed by placing the deceased in a combustible casket or container, that in turn, is placed in a cremation chamber and subjected to intense heat/flame. Bone fragments and dust are brushed from the chamber after cremation; however, it is impossible to remove all of the cremated remains. Because some dust and residue always remain in the chamber, there may be an inadvertent or incidental commingling of residue from previous cremations. This also may occur as a result of mechanically processing cremated remains.

Cremated remains may be buried, entombed, placed in a niche, scattered over private land with permission of owner or over public property (may require permit), or remain in family's possession, usually in an urn (wood, marble, or metal container).

Cremated remains should be collected upon notice of availability. The crematory authority may dispose of the remains in a legal manner 120 days after the cremation or after agreed to pick-up date.

> —"Consumer Guide to
> Arizona Funerals Information,"
> Arizona State Board of
> Funeral Directors and Embalmers

Funeral Services for Helen Brown

CATEGORY A—SERVICES

Professional Services

Direct Cremation (Non-declinable) $1,000.00

Cremation Fee $300.00

Transportation

Transfer of Remains to Funeral Home—Vehicle $350.00

Service/Utility Auto $175.00

CATEGORY A—TOTAL $1,825.00

CATEGORY B - MERCHANDISE

Minimum Cremation Container $95.00

CATEGORY B—TOTAL $95.00

CATEGORY C—CASH ADVANCES

Copies of Death Certificate $150.00

Medical Examiner Permit $15.00

CATEGORY C—TOTAL $165.00

TOTAL A, B & C $2,085.00
SERVICES, MERCHANDISE AND CASH ADVANCES

STATE AND LOCAL TAXES $7. 56

BALANCE DUE $2,092.56

Required Disclosures:
Direct Cremation

A direct cremation (without ceremony) includes transfer of deceased within 50 miles; basic services of Funeral Director and Staff; refrigeration (for the first 24 hours); cleansing, handling and care of unembalmed remains; dressing; use of facility and staff for private viewing by next of kin (up to ½ an hour); and transportation to crematory, crematory fee (for processing time greater than 48 hours from time of arrangement conference, excluding weekends and holidays). If you want to arrange a direct cremation, you can use an alternative container. Alternative containers encase the body and can be made of materials like fiberboard or composition materials (with or without an outside covering). The containers we provide are cardboard (with no pillow or bedding), basic container (totally combustible containers) include pillow, bedding and with or without fabric covering, Hardwoods (either natural or stained finish) with crepe or velvet interior.

This package includes Paradise Memorial Crematory, Inc.'s cremation fee.

The deceased Helen Brown
Will be held at Messinger Indian School Mortuary
7601 East Indian School Road, Scottsdale, Arizona
Until final disposition.

Melissa Pritchard
(Print Name of Responsible Party)
Date 4-06-08
Time 16:45

Hawthornden Castle
Lasswade, Midlothian
Scotland

—Ut honesto otio quiesceret

SOON AFTER THE DEATH OF MY MOTHER, I found myself at an international writer's retreat held in a Scottish castle named Hawthornden, an hour outside of Edinburgh. A short walk from the castle, part of a 120-acre woodland estate running alongside the River North Esk, is the cave that sheltered Sir William Wallace, the Scottish hero made famous stateside by Mel Gibson's portrayal in the film *Braveheart*. Hawthornden Castle is part fifteenth-century ruin with a warren of Pictish caves below it, carved of red sandstone and said to have hidden King Robert the Bruce, Bonnie Prince Charlie, and William Wallace. The habitable L-shaped half of the castle was built in the seventeenth century by Sir William Drummond, Cavalier poet and friend of Ben Jonson, Michael Drayton, and other literary figures of his age. Hawthornden Castle has been an international writers retreat since 1982, and the writers, selected several times a year for monthlong residencies, live in rooms, working behind doors marked Boswell, Brontë, Herrick, Jonson, Evelyn, Shakespeare, Yeats.

In filling out my application months before, I had whimsically requested the use of a typewriter. Because of the noise such an antiquated machine would presumably make, I was separated from the row of writers' rooms on the third floor, rooms accessed by a staircase as tightly spiraled as a nautilus shell. I was put into private quarters on the second floor reached by a short climb from the first. The name on my door was Shakespeare.

I had come to Scotland to write, but I had also come to grieve. Our culture is skittish about mourning, impatient and awkward with bereavement's uneven process. Friends had been exceptionally kind, but the overall message I had gotten from society, the environment at large, was make haste, move on, pay bills, earn your keep.

Shakespeare. My wailing room, done in dark red, dark green, and ivory, housed a benign monster: an immense, pillared, wood-canopied bed hewn of heavy timber so old and dark it appeared black. On the headboard, formally painted in golden lettering, was the year 1651 and the initials, PH and MH. Set off by hand-carved floral and geometric patterns were human figures, two male, one at each end of the headboard, and one female, in the center, her arms crossed beneath her naked breasts, fingers encircling each erect, if slightly squared, nipple. The room had a manteled fireplace, a wardrobe, and a plain desk set before a large pair of paned windows overlooking a sea of forest, an unseen river, the North Esk, rushing along below, and above, a Gainsborough sky with shifting, scudding wreaths of silver and white cloud.

For the thirty days I lived in this room, the only sounds I heard (even better when I flung the windows wide so fresh, wind-scrubbed air could pour in) were birdsong—wrens, warblers, magpies, woodpeckers, kestrels, and others—the murmur of the Esk, and trees, an ancient woodland of oak, ash, and elm, and hawthorn, tossed by an occasional tempest of wind, leaves flashing white and green, a sound like rough surf. Gentler sounds came from the kitchen, directly beneath my room, when the Scottish housekeeper, Mary, prepared hot porridge and coffee in the morning, and later in the day, as the French cook, Alex, slid dishes out of cupboards, chopped vegetables, conducted a muted clatter of pots and pans, her efforts sending the tantalizing savor of what we were to dine on that night drifting up the curved stairway. The spark of guilt I felt, being given such private, spacious quarters because of a typewriter I would end up never using, was quickly extinguished. Given my suppressed mourning, my blanketing sadness, this room, away from the rest, was perfect.

The Reformation-era bed, the atmosphere, ascetic, no modernity beyond electric lights and decent plumbing—no e-mail or Internet, no phone, no television or radio, no cars—the quiet, the forest, the light—my books and my pens—my meals prepared (a basket of food left outside my door promptly at noon, a tea tray in the afternoon), laundry done, linens changed weekly—my only assignments to sleep, eat, walk, write (though no one ever inquired as to one's progress), and converse with four fellow writers during dinner and in the upstairs drawing room afterward, where we took up reading Thomas Hardy's *The Mayor of Casterbridge*, eager, each evening, for the self-induced tragedy of Michael Henchard—this cradled way of life, a childhood without chores, I called it, became a place where sorrow unveiled itself. A place thick with tales of Picts and Celts, Romans, druids, fairies, Knights Templar, grand master Freemasons, Gypsies, and the pagan Green Man, with castles and ruins of castles, forests with paths wending along rivers, steep precipices, meadows pearled with sheep and lambs, lanes flanked by wild rose, foxglove, saxifrage, horsetail, bluebells. Ghosts presided, too, lively and miasmic, haunting chapels and caves, appearing on forest footpaths and in Hawthornden Castle. Spirits disporting themselves as misty presences, as lights going on or off, doors opening and closing on their own, and once—we all saw it—a lamp flying across the drawing room. In my state of loss, I found such capricious afterlife cheering.

Shakespeare. My first night, I fell into a quarter sleep (the birds, still singing? the light, why so much?) tempered by a soft incredulity at my good fortune. My second and third and fourth nights passed in sporadic weeping, harsh bursts of grieving. Womb of my own dear self, source and friend, my petty quarrel and perpetual conflict, the one I had grown so intimate with in those final, terrible months, she was *gone*, a common word that had assumed grave, terrible, stony weight. Gone. Vanished. Gone. Invisible. Gone. No more. Gone. Incorporeal. Gone. Departed. Gone. Disappeared. Anglo-Saxon, *gan*. As if she had never been. There was nowhere on this earth I could ever again go to find her. She was ash in my home now, powdered and tamped into a hideous shoe-polish box, weighing little more than a feather and slipcovered in a purple velvet pouch, reminiscent of Crown Royal liquor pouches, something a member of the mortuary staff had solicitously handed her to me in. My father's body, cremated by the same mortuary five years before, had not been pouched; his squared remains, as brown as his surname, *dad in a box*, had been handed to me inside of a white shopping bag. Lord and Taylor. As if he were a purchase, which in some sense and by then, he was. I mentioned this to the mortuary staffer, confessing, too, that I had stashed my boxed father behind my six published books, hidden him in my library these past five years. As a result, I was given a velvet pouch for him, too. I left the mortuary, my mother tucked (my, what square, hard edges you have!) into the crook of one arm, the royal purple pouch for my father in my summer straw purse. Driving out of the parking lot while calling one of my daughters on the phone, I would have been immediately killed had not my other daughter, in the car with me, shouted for me to stop before we were slammed into by an oncoming, speeding four wheeler. We laughed—yes, like hyenas!—at the idea of being killed exiting a mortuary, one dead mother already in the car.

My parents, bagged in grape velvet, like tacky purple stuffed animals, sit side by side (sit? repose? lounge? tumble bumble? decay? What does one say of dust and knobs and shards in a box?) in an otherwise empty chest of drawers in the guest room, guests now, awaiting their flight to Honolulu, where, in an outrigger canoe ceremony (as they had requested), my sister and I will sift them like ingredients, blend them into the kelpish, blue-green broth of the Pacific.

I, on the other hand, am loath to let go. Can I not keep some little of their ashes, comingled? ("We are such stuff as dreams are made on . . . ") But in what? Where? And why? All at once, the logic of earthly interment is apparent, a specific place to visit, to show up to on holidays and bring flowers, to erect a granite stone or marble pillar or angel. A family gathering spot, a somber picnic ground. But my parents were not religious in any conventional sense, they were affluent gypsies, and in this age of global warming and impending environmental catastrophe, burial in the ground is passé, outdated, wasteful of precious space and vanishing hardwoods. Cremation has environmental cachet; ash is green, even if it lends itself to moments of Beckettian absurdity and comic pathos, like Jack, my mother's teddy bear. For the five years she flailed miserably on after my father's death, Jack kept her company, a teddy bear in a blue Hawaiian shirt with a plastic baggie holding a few thimblefuls of my father's ashes sealed up where the bear's imaginary heart would be. He was with her at the end, snuggled beside her in a hospital bed, his little eyes gleaming loyally, if blindly, his ash heart thumping for her, his Hawaiian shirt faded, and at her demise, at her dissolution, at her burning, her auto-da-fé, Jack was there, too, turning to flame in her enfolded, emaciated arms.

Father, Mother, Childe Forlorne

Rosslyn Chapel

One night, in the drawing room at Hawthornden, I heard the story of Hardy, how his heart was cut out of his corpse, kept first in a biscuit tin, then interred at the cemetery he had requested his body be buried in (the rest of Mr. Hardy went to Westminster Abbey, sadly demonstrating the plight of being torn asunder, like a saint or martyr, by one's own fame). In the section of the church known as the Lady Chapel is the earliest known stone-carved *danse macabre*, sixteen human figures each dancing with a skeleton. Every inch of this chapel is obsessively carved with Christian symbols as well as gargoyles, Norse dragons, angels playing bagpipes, Lucifer tied and hanging upside down, and over one hundred Green Men, male faces sprouting foliage, a symbol of fertility. Rosslyn Chapel is a book in stone, written in Celtic, Masonic, Templar, Pythagorean, gnostic, alchemical, and biblical texts. The real Stone of Destiny is rumored to be buried in the chapel, as is the Holy Grail and shards of the Black Rood, or True Cross, carried from the Holy Land by William "the Seemly" Sinclair. Christ's mummified head is said by some to be hidden inside the famous Apprentice Pillar; these tales abound and inspire theories, one wilder than the next. Stories of the devil's chord, of an astral doorway, of UFO sightings around Rosslyn have given the tiny chapel a supernatural charisma attracting thousands of visitors. I am a visitor, too, and Rosslyn Chapel, with its *danse macabre*, is more than a site of religious miracle and mystery. It is my second (silent) wailing room. Its graves, its symbols, speak of resurrection, of the infinite many gone into the dark.

Hawthornden Castle

Where better to grieve than in the same castle where a famous Scottish poet, William Drummond of Hawthornden, born December 13, 1585, mourned as well? He grieved the loss of his parents, Sir John Drummond and Susannah Fowler; he mourned poor Miss Cunningham of Barnes, his betrothed, who died on the eve of their wedding. He married, much later in life, a Miss Elizabeth Logan, because she bore a tender resemblance to Miss Cunningham, and of their nine children, six perished, giving him more occasion for grief. Drummond's fine sonnets, still subjects of scholarly research, all carry the strain, the gentle rumination upon death in them, an emphasis we might find morbid today, insulated as we are by the near promise of a medically induced old age. But Drummond lived in a time when death's gait evenly paced, if not outpaced, life's. What better spot to mourn than in the castle of a poet known for his many epitaphs and sonnets composed for departed friends, a poet who, thinking himself near death at age thirty-five, wrote to his good friend Sir William Alexander a sonnet ending with these lines:

> *Here Damon lies, whose songs did sometimes grace*
> *The murmuring Esk: may roses shade the place!*

His famous prose piece, "The Cypress Grove," a mystical meditation on death, was written in a cave inside a forest alive with roe deer, red foxes, pheasant, rabbits, squirrels, and badgers, near green meadows wandered over by horses, sheep, and cattle, in green, rain-swept air thick with stories of battles with Romans and Norsemen, of the Crusades, their monks and knights and ladies, of brutal warfare with the English for freedom, of druidic wisdom, the teachings of the Celts still whispering if one stops to listen, in the ancient, black-limbed oaks, the gorse and Scotch broom, the flowering hawthorn, wild rose and foxglove, the springing leap of roe deer, or the hoarse, raucous chorus of ravens, all of which accompany me on each daily walk, walks as healing as *Shakespeare*, with its bed, its desk, its silence, its green view, the comforting sounds, beneath my feet, of food being prepared, nurturance delivered to the minds and souls of the resident writers, this writer, laboring, sorting her way to sanity, solitary, *danse seule*, in *Shakespeare*.

Rosslyn Chapel

A poem of stone . . . powdered with stars.

—Thomas Ross

I have walked fast this morning, beneath a childhood sky of bright enameled blue. I left Hawthornden late, so I must walk fast, three kilometers through woodland glen and meadow, to be at the chapel for the Eucharist at 10:30. I arrive barely in time, hot from an hour's walking, smelling of boiled wool from my green sweater, my hair turning to sheep's wool.

The service, preceded by organ music, is old fashioned, sedate, as though we have all day, and the hymns we sing, found in our faded hymnals, are by George Herbert; Alfred, Lord Tennyson; William Blake ("For Mercy has a human heart / Pity a human face"). . . . In the organ loft above us, the morning's psalm is sung in plainchant by a unseen parishioner. Even in June, the stone chapel is bleakly cold, and the flames of white candles waver from unseen drafts. It is easy to float backward centuries and see the chapel broken into, seized as a stable for Cromwell's warhorses when he laid siege to nearby Rosslyn Castle, to smell the sweat, dung, and straw, to hear the rough shouts and curses of soldiers, rather than the sweet singing of a dwindled, aging congregation of Scottish Episcopalians.

The grace of history, the dead, are those I feel most kin to now. The living seem removed, through no fault of theirs, they are meant to live and to savor all they can, and there will be that again for me as well, but for now I am more at home with the dead, with those who grieve, or with those who remember, with the reverend, and the lay reader, as I cup my hands to receive the Eucharist, kneeling at the altar, below the statue of Mary, placed there in the age of Victoria. Layers comfort me. We walk upright a while, then are divided, the lute from the player, the flesh returns to the sea or the earth or the air, the spirit becoming, perhaps, light. A friend said of my mother, weeks before she died, she is scattering into light. He was exactly right, and that is what we are all doing, though more slowly now than she—scattering into light, in line to take our greater place, to be those distant stars, or a presence on the stair, unseen but felt, or that splashy, violet bloom of azalea, or that midnight call of owl or nightingale, or that uneven fringe of cerise light on the horizon, or that deer, springing silent into the glen, or that pheasant, startled, flushed from its hedgerow, or the black church cat, William, winding himself around the legs of the reverend as he gives his Sunday announcements, his "adverts," for the church barbecue that afternoon, or for the archbishop of Brazil soon to visit, for this is the cat's home, too, this chapel. We kneel above nine knights in the chapel vault, unopened for centuries . . . the story goes that when the vault was opened, and a small party went down to see, someone touched the first knight, laid out in his armor, a bell, a candle, and a book beside him, and the body, at the touch, inside its metal casing, fell to dust. The others were left undisturbed, the vault was sealed, I kneel this Sunday, June 15, Father's Day, my knees resting over the dust and bones of the Saint Clair Knights Templar, five generations, my head bowed by the weight, growing lighter, of my own mortality, aging communicants on either side of me, devout Scottish worshippers, growing lighter, too, as they keep their weekly covenant of flesh and blood, as the notes of "Ave Maria" soar like sweetest birdsong above our head, the sounds of Katherine Longville, of Huguenot ancestry, mother of three, her boys home with their father, singing "Ave Maria" just as she had sung it the Sunday before for the wedding of a local couple, young Katherine Longville, who manages to keep up with her singing lessons every fortnight, for her boys, she says, are growing fast, and she too, is only here a while. We are all engrailed.

In the woods where Drummond wrote, I write. Along mossy paths in the woodland glen where he walked, I walk. Where hearts were carved out of flesh, thus is my heart carved from my own chest, and carried, by me, to the chapel at Rosslyn, to be laid down, laid down, too, in the cemeteries I walk between, a permanent seeding of graves on either side, I, the living creature, sailing between so many dead with all the pride of uprightness, straight-up-ness, of breath, motion, thought, my gay distinction from poor them, poor dead, sorrily prone and purblind. Yet with my grandparents gone, aunts and uncles gone, parents gone, mother most recently, with all gone and but one sister living, my privilege narrows, my distinction dims, my allegiance shifting to those on either side of me, rather than to those walking all around me, strolling on a fair Saturday in June, families, visitors, the young, all of us on our way, pilgrims threading the path between two graveyards, to Rosslyn Chapel.

Between Two Graves

Death is the sad estranger of acquaintances, the eternal divorcer of marriage, the ravisher of children from their parents, the stealer of parents from their children, the interrer of fame, the sole cause of forgetfulness, by which the living talk of those gone away as of so many shadows, or fabulous paladins.

—William Drummond, "The Cypress Grove"

Written in Stone

Lead, kindly light
At rest until He come
Sadly missed

A Thimble of Dust

In Loving Memory of
Helen, aged 9 and ½
And
Alexander Simmons
Aged 8
Who were tragically drowned in
The South Esk
On 26th August 1932

In memory of Jemima Arnott
Accidentally killed in an
Explosion at Roslin Gunpowder Mills
17th June 1925
Aged 20 years

Guy Justly
The dearly loved child
Of Colonel Oliver and Mary Nicholls
At Rosebank, Rosslyn
26th February, 1850
Aged 7 months
"Of such is the kingdom of heaven"

Certain names catch at us. Christina Grieve. Tibbie Porteous. Fanny Law. Euphemia Todd. Proudfoot. Or an advertisement at the bottom of one monument: Gibb Bro's. Roslin Granite Works, Aberdeen. It isn't fair. We pause, our imaginations held, by the special tragedy of young deaths, or the mixed triumph of old deaths (the oldest of both cemeteries, a woman, aged 102 years), or by the waste of the young in wars, or by parents left to grieve a child, or by the young husband left to grieve his wife, by the young killed in accidents, by disease, drowned. Less dramatic births and deaths, those whose dramas are recessed, we pass by. The sheer numbers of the dead render us frugal, we portion out sympathies.

> *Here Lye*
> *Anne Watson spouse of*
> *John Sturrock merchant*
> *In Edinburgh, Who died*
> *The 17the of May 1782*
> *Aged forty years*
> *Underneath this stone Doth as . . .*
> *Could . . . which . . .*
> *Alive did vigor . . .*
> *To . . . beauty as could . . .*

What is it that draws us to linger over half-ruined inscriptions, puzzling out dates, to the romance of old cemeteries, stones sunk, overtipped, inscriptions blurred to unreadability, moss, scabs of lichen and rotting leaves overtaking the imperturbability of marble, the endurability of granite? One gravestone, fallen to the ground, is so covered over by an inch or more of grass and buttercup, a thick green hide, it could be mown. Near it, an angel of marble, once celestially white, soaring upward, now gray and black, tipping sideway and hidden beneath an overgrowth of hawthorn, a Cadbury biscuit wrapper, obscenely prosaic, by its base. All this is homily in stone, all this, what we are coming to ourselves, those of us who stroll with solemn pleasure among the dead, finding poetry in the biblical or sentimental or stark inscriptions on the stones, yet glad, too, to end our reverie, close the iron gate, and walk the graveled hill back up to the chapel or inn or tea shop, glad to turn our thoughts from a sweet melancholic ramble to our appetites, our calendars, our health, our families and friends, the petrol level in the car, the need for a drink or to take a child, or ourselves, to the bathroom. We need to pee, or to kiss and hold hands, or to help Grandmother into the car, for we are, with thrilling vengeance, alive.

> *This Passive Place a Summer's nimble mansion,*
> *Where Bloom and Bees*
> *Exists an Oriental Circuit,*
> *Then cease like these—*

—Emily Dickinson

Last Sunday, walking along the river path to Rosslyn, I came upon an injured magpie. It had tucked itself into some leaves by the side of the path, and as the sun broke over the soft, green maple leaves, and with the rush of the river nearby, it seemed a not ungentle place to die. The earth is made of the dust of creatures who lived before. We walk carelessly upon the dead, the world a rounded grave.

> Mother, Father, Childe Forlorne
> All this has laid a softness around my grieving.

In those last hours, my mother's laboring to die seemed like my own fight, as a younger woman, to give birth. The inescapability of it, the solitude, no matter who was there, the sense of magnitude. I wanted to know, to ask if it was like giving birth, this prising apart of the flesh and the soul, but something stopped me—reserve, fear, lack of temerity, respect for my mother's profound passage. When it was time for the hospice nurses to help, when I mentioned the seeming labor in this dying business, they said, oh yes, we think of ourselves as helping to birth people into the afterlife. Like midwives? Yes. Like that.

And I worried. For the eleven months she had lived after the stroke, my mother, paralyzed, smart as ever and fully conscious, could speak but one word. *Yes*. Even when she meant no. We communicated telepathically, or through touch, or my bad jokes, which made her laugh, or with her eyes and her *yes* and my prattling on. Was sitting with her, watching documentaries like *Winged Migration, The Wild Parrots of Telegraph Hill*, or *10 Questions for the Dalai Lama* on my laptop, or my taking her out into the care center's garden in her wheelchair, enough? Was spooning bits of whipped cream with chocolate sauce into her mouth—the last thing she ever ate—enough? Was washing her face with a warm then cool washcloth, combing her sparse hair, putting aloe vera Chap Stick on her lips, massaging her temples and earlobes, then rubbing lavender lotion on her face and hands, enough? Were these the proper rituals for death's handmaiden? Love made me clumsy, tripping after the one who led the dance.

Hours before her heart stopped, my mother bolted half up from her bed, where she had been resting, struggling to breathe from the pneumonia, and grabbed hold of my sister's hand, staring at her with a look of terror my sister later refined, upon reflection, as a look that said, "Is this it, then? Is this death?" It was an intense, eyes-wide-open look, and the violent grip on my sister's hand, the strength of this frail, eighty-pound woman, a baby bird nested in white, industrially washed linen, was so painful, so tight, my sister would have had to pry her fingers off if she had needed to. A death grip? I asked. We looked at one another, newly understanding the phrase.

We didn't want her to be afraid, so we asked the hospice nurse to give her a bit of morphine, a drop under her tongue, sublingual. She visibly relaxed, closed her eyes. Dozing, one might say, but for the struggle going on, the battle being lost. My sister tried to read a book she had brought; I tried to grade student essays. Who were we fooling?

When she opened her eyes twenty minutes later, we had music on, something she liked, instrumental, spiritual. I stood over her, smiling, and picked up her left hand, the paralyzed one, all bone now, and swung it gently back, forth, up, back, forth, up, as though we were waltzing. We're dancing, Mamma, I said. She smiled, then gave me a twinkling, openly flirtatious glance I remembered from childhood, the look she wore at parties, the look that had drawn so many young men to court her before I was ever born, and then, surprise upon surprise, my mother winked at me, a girl with all the world before her.

I leaped for the phone when it rang at 3:00 a.m. I woke my sister, who somehow already knew. I had wanted to be there, to hold her in my arms, to murmur to her like a lover. (I felt. I wanted. I!) Her greatest fear, she once told me, was of dying alone. But she hadn't died alone, had she? We had all been there in the days preceding, and a nurse she'd liked, whose name I can't recall, was with her as she "passed" (the current euphemism). The hospice nurses say it is extremely common for people to "take their journey" (another expression) when everyone has gone home, has left the room. When we are with them, we hold on too hard, we won't let them go.

We drove the ten minutes to the care center, no traffic, the hour before dawn, took the elevator to the third floor, turned right past the dining hall then left down the hall to her room. Helen Brown said the sign by her door, a symbol beside it that meant danger of falling. (They used to find her on the floor, having rolled somehow out of her bed; so they lowered her bed each night so that it was only an inch or so from the floor, and put gym mats down to cushion her fall.)

The overhead fluorescent lights were on (ugh! turn them off!); flowers bloomed on the windowsill, stargazer lilies. The artificial Christmas tree from Walgreens I had put up five months before and never taken down because I thought the colored lights and shiny ornaments added some cheer, and because I did not know what else to do with it, was there. The black-and-white photograph of her great-grandmother Zadrow, her grandmother Fredericka, her mother, Rose Louise, and herself, little Helen Lorraine, five years old, hung above her bed.

She lay on her back in an overwashed gown of faded blue, her mouth gaping open. My sister said, can't we ask them to close her mouth? We went to the nurse's station, asked, and were told they had tried, but that her jaw, loose now, as happens with death, kept falling open. We pulled the bedsheet up over the mouth that frightened us.

I asked for time alone with her. Corpse? *Mater Magnificat*? Oh, Mamma. I knelt by the bed, fell to my knees before the altar of my mother. I sensed her spirit, free, prised loose, and spoke aloud. I wept. I kissed her cheek, stroked her fine, soft hair. I went back to the nurse's station, asked for scissors, came back and snipped a lock of her hair, tinted light brown, her weekly hair appointment a last feminine pleasure.

> *And death shall have no dominion.*
> *Dead men naked they shall be one*
> *With the man in the wind and the west moon;*
> *When their bones are picked clean and the*
>   *clean bones gone,*
> *They shall have stars at elbow and foot . . .*

> —Dylan Thomas

When I was fifteen, my mother, who knew I wrote poetry and burned Chinese incense in my room but did not know how many times I rode my bicycle to the cemetery behind our house and wandered with solemn pleasure among the graves, gave me, for Christmas, a collection of poems by Dylan Thomas. I imagine her choosing this book for me, wanting to please me. She was not a literary person, she did not read poetry, yet she made the gesture within herself to understand my nature. She wrote, rather formally, in red ink, "A Merry, Merry Christmas to our girl, with love from Mother and Dad."

A female Anna's hummingbird appeared in my garden the day after her death. It hovered outside my study window, looking in at me for a long, suspended time. It came back the next day and the next, hovering before that same window as I sat at my desk. And one final time, as I sat in my garden, praying to her to show me a sign that she was free now and approved of how I was handling all the earthly details of life, for I was missing her terribly and falling under my burdens, the hummingbird appeared, this time hovering, hanging in the air inches from my face. It stayed for a very long time. The next day, I hung a feeder in the tree outside my study window, but it had disappeared. There had been no hummingbirds in my garden before and none since.

According to Tibetan Buddhist teachings, the spirit has enough energy during the first hours and days after death to give signs to the living, but after that, the spirit moves on, signs fade, then are gone. *Gan.* My mother loved birds and fed them all, especially her elusive, iridescent hummingbirds.

The day before she died, I gave her two bouquets of star-gazer lilies, pink striped, perfumed trumpets, the last blooms she would ever see. One month later, a clairvoyant came up to me and said, I see your mother has tiny little birds flying all around her—hummingbirds!—also, she says to thank you for the lilies you gave her, they have always been her favorites.

Mommy. Mamma. *Gan.*

> *Journeying through the world*
> *To and Fro, To and Fro,*
> *Cultivating a Small Field*

—From the gravestone of
Joanna Dun, 1634
Lasswade Cemetery
Midlothian, Scotland

A Graven Space

A HAGIOGRAPHIC MIST BLURS Georgia O'Keeffe, somewhat like those specious clouds put forth by the theater's notable fog machine. Certain individuals seem fated in life or posthumously to be transfigured into myth, their humanity sacrificed to the mystic process. I suspect the reverence enshrouding Ms. O'Keeffe, suspect the worshipful tendency in myself. There is danger in selectively evoking a life, deliberately arranging events and statements to conjure some saint of the unattainable achievement, some icon at a remove from the rest of us. We are happy to create the graven image; it distracts us from ourselves.

As I began to read about Georgia O'Keeffe, to study the open paintings, the cryptic life, as biographies and photographs lent various lights, I tumbled quickly, as hushed and awed as anybody else. Doubtless I was inspired by her as a role model, for she has given women rare leave and courage to claim space and light and time as artists. Yet as her heroic stature enlarged, she seemed to me humanly misplaced. I admired and took strength from her; I did not particularly like her. As legend accumulated, her human substance receded; the more I wrote glowingly, worshipfully of the example, the virtue, the brilliance, the feminist ideal, the more remote, inaccessible she seemed. The thing grasped eludes us.

At this frustrated point, I came upon a photograph of Georgia O'Keeffe wearing a black, mandarin-collared shirt, holding close to her face, delicately held between those famous hands, a scissored run of paper dolls. She was grinning at all us worshipers. Then I looked again and no, she was not smiling; her expression was enigmatic, androgynous as she held a dry length of spinal column, like parched, oversimple lace, between her hands. I took my visual misperception as a clue. This woman, what I knew and had culled from details of her life, from the myriad bright and dull things netted from a fluid existence, surely, I hoped, that beneath the arid self-reliance, heroic independence, and artistic genius, lay humor, levity, wit gone to giddiness.

I read how she and her sister walked at twilight across the frying-pan flat Texas plains, tossing bottles at the sky and shooting them down, exploding the thick glass with bullets. I liked her for that. She painted in a shack up at Lake George in the nude and screamed at inquisitive children when they came, rather naturally, to spy on her. I liked that. She purchased a car in New Mexico and taught herself—recklessly, perilously inexpert—to drive. I liked that, too. She cultivated gardens, sewed clothing, wanted a child, endured losses and defeats, once threw a charred turkey out and fled Thanksgiving guests, once interred a despised marble bust in the Stieglitz garden. She proved as vulnerable, silly, and grieving as any of us.

There is reason to desanctify this woman. We burden someone with mystique in part to evade ourselves—not so much to honor them as to subtly devalue ourselves. Those individuals who splash their life's canvas hugely, exuberantly, more than the rest of us, too sadly hesitant in the shaping of our lives—this near deification of an extraordinary artist like Georgia O'Keeffe, the worshipful distancing that creeps insidiously into our innocent study and regard of her, comes from a reluctance to confront ourselves, our lives, an unwillingness to have faith in our own potential. The more we legend her up, trick her out in outrageous character, unsurpassable achievement, the more Promethean her proportions, the less we need to ask of ourselves. We hypnotize ourselves with her accomplishment, diminishing any need of our own, ask to be intimidated so we can remain in a familiar, if uncomfortable, state of perpetual self-disappointment—the dark side of admiration.

Humor acknowledges contradiction, and Georgia O'Keeffe was an artist of uncommon and cultivated paradox. Her chosen elusiveness provokes diverse interpretations, her renunciative stance reflects a profound engagement with the world. She went beyond prescribed female territory, confronting its symbols head on. The flower, so archetypically feminine, delicate, pale, passive, fragrant, fragile, she painted as fleshy, strong, vibrant, voluptuous, very nearly voracious. She set the white pelvis against the red female humps of the hill, and turned the body of the world, of ourselves, inside out.

Visionary exile, Georgia O'Keeffe turned from the world's quotidian gnawings and concerns. Many of us stay busy inventing reasons not to create—we complain, whine, and will not work because we are terrified of doing so. She was impatient with this: you do not wait for the perfect setting and mood to be artistic, you seize and breathe your air, lay guiltless, unequivocal claim to the light, the space, the aloneness. You pioneer the unknown, the edges of definition and beyond, the cusp between the sky and the earth, that brilliant life cusp where humble and sacred touch. Not without loss, she forsook much of what we consider human paths to fulfillment—romantic love, traditional marriage, motherhood—and went on to invent her own universe, disturbing us with her potent, altered version of reality, giving us glorious, crucial leave to do the same. Yet we impede ourselves, prove the greatest obstacle.

If human life is about loss—the procession of growth, acquisition, and accumulation, that necessary relinquishment of childhood, naive faith, youthful health, perfect love, perfect children—then for selfish purposes I demystify Georgia O'Keeffe. I will not place her out of reach, will crank down the pedestal, touch the statue, and find it is a woman who could behave noxiously, act arrogantly and outrageously at close mortal range. She was no oracle we need cast our self-declared puny lives into. She broke the scale most of us restrict ourselves within and did so not without fear, but without fear stopping her. She confronted the relation between luminous spirit and humble form, shaped mortality into graven forms with colors suggestive of the infinite. She confronted sexuality, death, and loss, transmuted them, transcended them. She was spartan, stringent, voluptuous, monastic, sensuous, an inspiration at a distance, recalcitrant in person. Refusing definition, rejecting all theory, confounding any attempt to pin her down, even now she eludes us, like water, like sand. She made holy the simple. "The vision ahead may seem a bit bleak, but my feeling about life is a curious kind of triumphant feeling about—seeing it bleak—knowing it is so and walking into it fearlessly because one has no choice—enjoying one's consciousness."

Rather than idolize Georgia O'Keeffe, making of her some reliquary for deceptive speculation, we would do well to return to ourselves and, strengthened by her example, get on with it. Life. The curious triumph of loss. Love.

Decomposing Articles of Faith

IN WHICH SISTER PRITCHARD, Scribbler Pritchard, Goody Pritchard holds forth:

Praise God

That God both does and does not uphold our Neighborhood Watch.

That God both is and is not a projection of our innermost desires and fears.

That God is a handyman, our prayers to Him a honey-do.

From Whom All Blessings Flow . . .

A golden arabesque

An opium scheme.

I believe in God the Father Almighty

Karma: man's howl for justice indefinitely extended.

Reincarnation: man's fixed quest for immortality, a variant of fear.

Man's/woman's wish, the peoples' wish—gender induces hobbled language.

Maker of Heaven and Earth

Samuel Beckett remembered his mother's womb, even its color.

I recall being hanged on some medieval gallows.

I met a soul mate in Prague last summer—a Pakistani diplomat who claimed his hands had been cut off in a former life and that he had known me for lifetimes. I insisted my head had been cut off in a former life with the result that in this life, I have been afraid to speak up for years, and I have a hysteric's loathing of necklaces and neck scarves. Perhaps in one of our lifetimes together, I quipped drily, you lacked your hands and I was minus my head. Oh yes, most definitely, said the kindly, if not kingly, Pakistani man, lubriciously rubbing together his attached hands.

We believe what makes us happy. I am happiest believing in God, not so much the Singular deity, the divinely molded One, but a permeable, porous, timeless, palpable outside-the-law essence informing all things high and low. God as good vibration.

Of All That Is Seen and Unseen

Swimming in the pool yesterday morning, I came upon a small sickle-shaped eucalyptus leaf floating on the water's turquoise surface. The leaf was blackened with hundreds of ants, the leaf their life raft. I picked the leaf out of the pool, laid it on the ledge, and studied its miniature horrorscape—the ants on the bottom layers were clearly deceased, the ones at the top, a few, not many, were still alive. Survivors. How had this tragedy unfolded, how did hundreds of ants—and were they of the same tribal declension?—wind up on a eucalyptus leaf pale and hooked as a nail paring, and what of me, their deity, come upon them, rescuing those still alive—would they tell stories of me, of the great wet-head, chlorine-scented deity who saved them? Will religions and subreligions be built around their extinguished memory of me? Is that how God looks down upon us Wee Willie Winkees on earth, ants heaped on a curving leaf in various stages of fornication, a-sup, a-reveling, a-death, and a-dying?

God from God

I deplore the lack of universal compassion in our species. I issue from a draconian line of philosophers that says if one suffers, we all suffer; if one fails, it is the fault of all.

I am as culpable as the rest, my veneer spit shined and shallow, my intentions on the level of a Sufi master's. Pill and pearl. Twee of divine.

Look how my articles of faith are disheveled, disorderly, squalling, nailed to no door, unrecitable, in bloody flux, forgettable.

Light from Light

Yet I believe them, my faith's restless articles.

It seems I have passed through compassion fatigue into Al Qaeda/Taliban fatigue, into *The Secret* fatigue, mantra fatigue, gospel fatigue, chatter and Twitter fatigue, silence fatigue, God fatigue, gratitude fatigue, high-minded fatigue, porn and news fatigue. Beyond fatigue, I am full of great, good thanks to be, however long my spark lasts, alive.

True God from True God

My dog most certainly is *god* spelled backward. He is sublimely present. No fatigue. He loves. He licks. He chases and wags. Eats, shits, leaps like a dolphin for his Frisbee. Sleeps and guards. Snorts in his sleep and awake, begs for orts of cheese, smackerels of beef crumb. A belly rub, an ear massage.

I have seen miracles happen. It is true, I manifest people, events, money. It may be that I want to be superior in a moral yet humble way that others will admire.

The self: unredeemable, worthy of parsed, parsnip worship.

Begotten, Not Made

Vexing! So many articles of faith that do not cohere. They are infinite, these articles of faith, yet now I have article fatigue and must stop creating them.

Hear this: I believe in God and have moments of sublimity, of visionary migraine halo, most often during Sunday five o'clock Mass at Mount Carmel Church when I sit among the lame, the halt, the blind, those who are homeless, those on their ventilators, beside the mentally ill man who rushes up to be first to receive the host, always wearing his red suspenders, knees quaking. O Holy is their Queen.

The priest is pro-life and drives me nuts-o with his fiery complacency about things. I wonder if he dreams of being a lover, a husband, a chef, a toy maker, a defender of auto-da-fé.

Hail Mary Full of Grace

The figure hanging above his head is what matters. No one listened then. No one listens now. Søren Kierkegaard said no one can truly follow the word of Jesus. It is too hard, he said. The people are not willing.

The Lord Is with Thee

We send up our saints like Venetian fireworks then plow them under mud and offal. We hate and worship them because they are not us. They are the Goody Two-Shoes in third grade we loved to torment but in our beds, alone at night, envied.

Blessed Art Thou amongst Women

I once knelt beside Mother Teresa's marble tomb in Calcutta. A force field clamped onto me, I swooned, lost all sense of time and space. I was caught up in something greater than myself. I longed to stay there until I died but didn't want to be thought of or discovered as mad. I was afraid of this power I encountered.

And Blessed Is the Fruit of Thy Womb, Jesus

I once met a nun who ran Mother Teresa's home for the dying. She lived inside an egg-shaped aura, a glow, a holy substance that everyone grew tame and pie mouthed around.

I once met a Buddhist saint, a former jazz singer and beauty who levitated, laughed airily, and had just spent hours in Thailand with the Dalai Lama. She explained the history of the relics I was studying in the Tibet House. This was in New Delhi. Bald, wrapped in white, she called herself the humble messenger, and in the gift shop, bought a calendar for a friend.

Holy Mary, Mother of God

There is a God who is a cloud of unknowing.

Pray for Us Sinners

On my knees, I behave. Am better. Quieter.

Now

Take me.

And At the Hour of Our Death

I am hardwired for paradise.

Naked and un-alone.

Amen.

Finding Ashton

WHEN I WAS NINE, I ran away. I was soon discovered a few blocks from home by a supercilious, sneering neighbor boy nobody much liked named Eddie. He marched me back to my mother but not before the shock of that short freedom, the vastness of the world, and the mixed mercies of people caring about me had all made a deep impression.

Now I was running again, this time from my own life. On the fifth anniversary of my father's death, my mother had suffered a stroke that left her paralyzed; she died ten months later, in April 2008. I flew to Hawaii that autumn and scattered handful after handful of my parents' mingled dust into the Pacific Ocean they had loved.

Death, I discovered, uncorks sentimentality. I made myself throw out the pair of shoes my dad had been wearing the day he died (what was I going to do? bronze them? wear them?) though I kept a lock of my mother's dyed, pale brown hair. I had locks of my children's hair, too—two daughters now with homes of their own, lives of their own. I was a professor at a large university, a published novelist, a successful, self-sufficient woman. But waking up every morning to a large, empty house was a new, unexpected shriving. I felt as if my skeleton were gone, as if I had been filleted, deboned. I was standing, but barely. Wearing an exoskeleton of books, accomplishments, and titles, I fled to a children's poetry project in the brothels of Calcutta, then to an all-women's medical mission in Ecuador. After that, who knew? I was drawn to places of suffering that surpassed my own.

I didn't think about any of this rationally. This was not self-awareness. I was simply an old, old child orphaned by death, a mother with unneeded mothering skills, an ex-wife with decades of memories, not all of them bad. A woman bereft, floundering, ashamed of her weakness, fearful for her future, beginning with the next five minutes.

It was January 2009, and I had managed to keep my next destination and assignment, as an embedded journalist interviewing female soldiers, a secret from my daughters. With body armor purchased online, military-issue winter underwear, notebooks, tape recorder, vitamins, stale PowerBars, and a nagging conscience, I arrived at Bagram Airfield, forty-seven kilometers north of Kabul, and sent a quick e-mail from the media operations office, letting my children know I was now in Afghanistan, under the protection of the US Air Force. I would, I promised, be safely home in two weeks.

Under leaden winter skies, nine air force and army soldiers, bulky with gear and weapons, waited on rain-darkened gravel near tan, mud-splashed Humvees to begin the drive north to their small forward operating base (FOB) in Panjshir Province. The youngest, Air Force Senior Airman Ashton Goodman, twenty-one, stood beside me in camouflage uniform with pistol, carbine, knife, heavy boots, and helmet, explaining that as a vehicles op (short for vehicle operator dispatcher), she maintained and drove Humvees, Land Cruisers, "whatever has wheels." She added that she couldn't wait to drive one of the newer mine-resistant ambush-protected all-terrain vehicles, a Paleolithic-looking monster built to survive roadside bombs, improvised explosive devices (IEDs), and ambushes. A former supply-truck driver on mine-infested roads in Iraq, Goodman was about two months into her new deployment in this relatively peaceful, "model" province.

Established in 2005 by combined American military and civilian, and NATO forces, the Panjshir Provincial Reconstruction Team (PRT), working closely with the Afghan people, was responsible for diverse humanitarian efforts, from medical clinics and vaccination programs to schools and engineering and agricultural projects. Although at the time its seventy-member team was the smallest of the twenty-six PRT sites throughout Afghanistan, FOB Lion was considered a showcase. I was going there to write about the five female soldiers on that team.

My initial impression of the diminutive, blue-eyed, athletic Senior Airman Goodman that bleak afternoon at Bagram was of a wholesome GI Jane action figure come to life. She'd missed her dream of becoming a fighter pilot, she later told me, by being one inch under air force height requirement.

Vaulting lightly into the driver's seat of an armored Humvee, Goodman, as she liked to be called, secured her helmet and eye shield, adjusted her radio, and shouted a rallying cry, "All right, let's kick anus!" as we pulled out of Bagram, a three-vehicle convoy heading to FOB Lion, about 120 kilometers north, in the Hindu Kush Mountains. Goodman's acronym-laced patter over the radio, her belting out of lines from Jon Bon Jovi's "Never Say Die" ("I love that song," she says. "It pretty much defines my view of life: Never quit, death is just a part of life, and brotherhood and camaraderie are paramount") distracted me from morbid musings on the odds of our being blown up by an IED, a stark possibility made plain in an earlier briefing. When I wasn't trying to see out of the grimy porthole window, I was admiring Goodman's expert handling of her armored Humvee. IEDs, buried beneath roads, and vehicle-borne IEDs, often suicide bombs, were the main cause of military casualties in Afghanistan, but Goodman's courage and calm skill gave an illusion of safety. My survival was in her young hands.

It seemed unlikely this soldier and I would find any personal connection. Mine was a comfortable, private life of travel, writing, and teaching, hers, a life of service in a war zone, little privacy or comfort, a stringent, daily regimen of monotony and risk. We were generations apart. Yet in the five days I spent with Goodman, I found that beneath her veneer of military protocol and discipline, beneath her bravado, kill talk, and cussing, she was surprisingly vulnerable, coltish. She was also ravenous for adventure. As we drove from one PRT mission to the next in this harsh, mountainous province, visiting medical clinics, a fledgling radio station, a girls' school, an international aid drop, I learned she was earning a degree in biology, planned to be a veterinarian, was an amateur photographer and an aspiring author, writing "little stories," she said, to relieve stress. She had just started Rosetta Stone Spanish lessons and confessed to missing bubble baths. She had a tattoo on her left forearm, *Studium Nunquam Intereo*—"spirit never dies."

Wondering how much of Goodman's tough-girl act was a coping mechanism, I asked about the difficulties of being a young woman and a wartime soldier. "Balancing my femininity within a male-dominated military has actually posed a problem," she told me. "I always feel that I have to prove myself. It's like I have two personas: my butch military side and my dorky, girlie side—it's a constant struggle."

I had no doubt Goodman would prove fearless in battle, and it was humbling to know she would give her life to protect mine, a stranger's. Yet civilian life presented its own battles; it was from these, as well as her own self-doubt, that I wanted to protect her.

ON MY SECOND DAY IN PANJSHIR, headed back to FOB Lion after visiting a remote medical clinic in the district of Shutol, our two-vehicle convoy of military women and mujahideen guards was caught in a sudden blizzard. Navigating the dirt road, a slick, hairpin descent with snow falling and sticking faster than the windshield wipers could clear the glass, Goodman, jaw clenched, half-humming, half-singing a children's song, managed to keep the Land Cruiser from sliding off the road and plunging into a rocky ravine. Voicing concern about the less-experienced driver behind her ("He's got a wife and new baby at home"), she signaled that she was stopping, braked, then jumped out to help three elderly Afghan men standing beside a rust-eaten sedan, its grille nosed tight into an ochre cleft of the mountainside. Within minutes, Goodman freed the car. Politely thanking her, the men got back into their ancient vehicle and proceeded down the sinuous road, with Goodman, still humming, following behind.

On another day, we stopped for lunch at the only restaurant in Panjshir, a pale green, threadbare café on the riverside, serving typical Afghan fare—kebabs, pilaf, and a kind of nan I had never seen—the pieces huge and snowshoe shaped. Goodman grinned as she tore into hers—"I love this stuff," she said. At the end of our meal, the rest of us handed over all of our extra nan, which she happily wrapped in her hijab, the traditional Muslim head scarf the five US military women wore as a sign of cultural respect whenever they left the base. Each of the women had a collection of colorful scarves bought in local markets; during my visit, I was given a fringed, amber-colored hijab, which I still have.

Outside the restaurant, Goodman leapfrogged across rocks into the middle of the broad, taupe-colored Panjshir River to pose, mugging and clowning, for pictures. Driving back to the base, she hooted with delight whenever we passed a scatter of scruffy red hens pecking listlessly along the roadside or huddled in a dirt yard. Crazy about birds, especially chickens, she also lavished an almost impish affection on shunned creatures like slugs, frogs, and mice. She unabashedly mothered dogs, birds, babies of all kinds, anything innocent and sweetly alive, and it wasn't hard to imagine what a wonderful mother she would be. When I asked about her boyfriend, she said his name was David, David Flint, and that he was in the army, fighting in Afghanistan. Like her, he was from Indianapolis, and she couldn't wait to get back home to "raise a whole bunch of chickens" since David liked them, too. She didn't want to say much more, reluctant, perhaps, to jinx her future happiness.

On the fourth day, after hiking down a snowy mountain trail to another tiny medical clinic, we sat, five military women, a translator, and I, on floor cushions in an unheated mud-and-straw room, drinking tea with two doctors and a midwife in a black burka, discussing how many babies had been born since the PRT's last visit. Afterward, as we trudged single file back up to our vehicles, Goodman launched into a snowball fight. Everyone joined in, sniping snowballs at one another, until Goodman, cheeks burning pink, fell backward laughing, scissoring her arms and legs, making an angel, uneven and solitary against the flat expanse of snow.

Even when serious and quiet, Goodman blazed with uncommon energy. On the day before I left Panjshir to return to Bagram, she met me in the base's chilly community room, the last of the interviews for my magazine story. Minus weapons, with her golden-brown hair pulled back into a shiny, clubbed ponytail, she looked startlingly young, precociously mature, self-effacing yet eager for the novelty of being interviewed. As she answered questions about her decision to join the military and admitted her hope of being a published writer one day, I watched her surface toughness drop away, saw that she was no different from my own daughters, from the young women who were my university students. Like them, she was eager to create a life that mattered. In that paneled room with its black faux-leather furniture and an artificial Christmas tree, shorn of ornaments, keeping shadowy watch in one corner, a shy, sudden affection bloomed between us.

LATER THAT NIGHT, AFTER DINNER, she sat close beside me in the chow hall, examining photographs on my digital camera, images from recent trips to India, Scotland, Italy, France, England. As she asked about the people and places in the pictures, she confessed her desire to travel the world, to see it all—and the frank hunger and hope on her thoughtful, unmarked face moved me.

"Ashton, you're so young. You have lots of time."

Handing the camera back to me, she said, "I want to go to Africa."

After I returned home, we kept in touch. When I asked to read some of her work, she e-mailed two of her "humble writings," signing off with an embarrassed "Eek, Ashton." Emotional honesty was the hardest thing to teach writing students; her stories were bold, unflinchingly truthful. "You have an absolute gift," I wrote back. "I'm excited to read your books," she answered.

It was April now, springtime, and Ashton e-mailed photographs—an Afghan mother holding her newborn daughter, a puppy the soldiers had adopted, a pale, downy cluster of baby chicks, and panoramic views of the richly green, lush Panjshir Valley. In our interview, she had talked about her time in Iraq as a driver for line-haul convoys, routing supplies on IED-infested roads. "One of our guys was killed by a mine, and I was the first to know," she told me. "I wasn't supposed to tell anyone, so I was just walking around with this knowledge. After people were informed, I became one of the comforters. Afterward, it was really bad. We'd have to drive every day on the same road where it had happened, see the bomb hole, the trail of his blood. I went through a period of being really shaken up, stressed out, shaking, scared. Then I knew it was about fate, God, coincidence. When it was my time, it was my time. After that I wasn't scared." The most surprising thing about the mission in Panjshir, she went on, was how peaceful it was. She didn't have to be as guarded or as afraid of the people: "It's unlikely any of them has a bomb strapped to his chest."

Assigned by her PRT commander to serve on women's affairs, Ashton had begun attending weekly meetings, or *shuras*, with local Afghan women. She told me that she was impressed by their intelligence and tenacity. "It infuriates me that women here are treated as second-class citizens. I'd like to see a woman with her own shop, a woman doctor. It will take generations, though. They need infrastructure, schools, clean water, clean places to slaughter animals rather than by the side of the road. I'd really like to come back here in twenty years and show my kids how we helped."

Early in May, Ashton friended me on Facebook, a form of communication I was new to and ambivalent about, but willing to try. She added me to her personal e-mail list along with her parents, her little brother, Levi, and her boyfriend. We all got to read and congratulate her on her first publication, "Panjshir PRT Medics Improve Medical Sanitation," an article on the US Air Force Web site.

In a private e-mail, she described a brief trip home. "I did go on leave in March. It was a relief to get away, even though I love it here. The tension and stress were starting to get to me, and I was cranky and irritable. When I got back, I was my normal self again. The hardest part about being home was getting used to the complete freedom. I could wear what I wanted, shower without flip-flops, wear my hair down. I cried a lot, too. Home is a place for me to heal. It felt good to get it all out and have my mom hold me while I did. I'm still a momma's girl and always will be. Love, Ashton."

It was May 29, and I had worked all day on my article. I'd spent most of the afternoon revising, trying to capture Ashton's seemingly contradictory passion for Disney movies (her favorites were *The Little Mermaid* and *The Lion King*) and her tastes in music—techno, heavy metal, J-Pop (Japanese pop), and especially European power metal. "The lyrics are awesome because they always talk about being proud warriors like they're freaking ancient Celts fighting for the motherlands . . ."

Tired but still thinking about Ashton—had I gotten her right?—I went into my kitchen, began to scroll idly through Facebook, skimming the bright chatter of friends, before stopping cold at what had to be a callous joke, a notice posted by the Flanner and Buchanan Funeral Centers: Sr. Airman Ashton Lynn Marie Goodman, 21, of Indpls., died May 26, 2009, while serving in Afghanistan. She was born June 14, 1987 at Beale Air Force Base, CA. Ashton was in the U.S. Air Force 43rd Airlift Wing serving as a driver for Panjshir (Afghanistan) Provincial Reconstruction Team. She was a . . . Abruptly, the notice stopped. Beside it was an official air force photograph, stamp sized, of a barely recognizable Ashton, in dark blue dress uniform and peaked cap, looking like some nostalgic 1940s studio-lit version of herself. Numb with shock, I clicked over to her page to prove it was a joke, a mistake, but found only grieving messages from family, friends, her boyfriend. Crying now, frantically clicking for details, facts, calling a military friend in Afghanistan, calling local friends, still fastened to the Internet, I located the Department of Defense casualty list and found the official air force announcement saying that she had died near Bagram Airfield of wounds sustained from an IED.

I returned to her Facebook page, staring blindly at accumulating condolences. There were details of the funeral. The burial. Donations could be made to the World Wildlife Fund. Her father wrote that he had flown to Dover Air Force Base and "brought his pumpkin home." I responded with a short, stumbling sympathy note. I read every anguished message from David, fighting somewhere in Afghanistan, unable to attend Ashton's ceremony at Bagram Airfield, where her body was formally loaded onto a transport plane home.

> The moon is lonesome without you, but I look at it each
> night as it rises and see you staring back at me. I hope
> you are at peace. I miss you baby. Always fighting strong
> for your dreams, my little hummingbird.
>
> —David

My mother had always loved birds, especially hummingbirds. She had promised to send me a sign, once she passed, that her spirit was still alive; hours after her death, a hummingbird hovered at my window, looking in at me for an unmistakably long time. I called to my sister to come see this tiny, iridescent creature shimmering in midair, gazing at us through the glass, its wings beating up to eighty times per second, backward and forward, in the symbol for infinity. The hummingbird returned the next day and again on the third morning as I sat in the garden praying to my mother for help, for comfort—it came, jeweled messenger, shaking the air inches from my face before darting away. I never saw it again.

Ashton was killed less than three weeks before her twenty-second birthday. The birthday package David sent to Panjshir was returned, unopened. One of the first things he will do once he returns home to Indiana is find the tall pine tree

Ashton lies buried beneath and share with his little hummingbird the gift he had chosen to delight her.

Sometimes we run away to be reclaimed, to be reassured that if we are not wholly understood, at least we are loved. When I came home, my daughters let it be known how worried they had been, shocked and even hurt that their mother would go somewhere, anywhere, without asking or even telling them. I had left home like an impetuous child, wanting to be found. Instead I had found Ashton and was opened to love beyond my familiar given circle.

There are three photographs of Ashton I keep returning to. The first, taken days before her death, shows her sitting in a circle with Afghan women, wearing her favorite blue hijab, rain-like sparkles along the hem, her face turned to the camera, smiling serenely, as if telling the world she is glad to be fighting for justice with words now, not weapons. She looks like she does in most of her pictures—a bit indifferent to, or unsure of, her own prettiness. And it may have been the lighting, but in this photo, one of her last, she looks calm, radiant, ethereal.

Hardest to look at is the newswire image I came across online: Ashton's remains in a flag-draped transfer case being lowered from a transport plane at Dover Air Force Base.

Finally, there is the photograph she chose for her Facebook page: Ashton, balanced lightly on the edge of a cliff overlooking Panjshir Valley, arms raised high, lifted in a triumphant "Yes!" to life. Beneath the photo, this caption:

Don't forget to send me some love!!!! My address is Sr. Airman Ashton Goodman PRT Panjshir, APO AE 09354 I love getting cards and stuff in the mail. :):):):):)

"Still, God Helps You":
Memories of a Sudanese Child Slave

I T IS MONDAY MORNING IN PHOENIX, Arizona, and thirty-three-year-old William Mawwin is getting dressed for school. His right arm is an old prosthetic the color of Hershey's syrup. The prosthetic has begun to hurt him, but he cannot afford a new one. On his left hand, four fingers are missing down to the second knuckle. His naked back and chest are welted with raised, pinkish scars, some from beatings, others from burns. More scars, from knife wounds and skin grafts, map his body. In the slow, careful way he has taught himself, he puts on socks, jeans, a neatly ironed shirt, dress shoes with pointed tips. Across from his bedroom, a guest room stands empty except for a twin bed and a chest of drawers. His daughter's teddy bear sits propped on the pillow. William, who is six feet tall and slender, sometimes just sits on her bed and holds the stuffed bear.

He does not look forward to school holidays, to spring or winter breaks. Each day away from the classroom lengthens his exile, leaves openings for bad memories. He takes the public bus to school or, if he is short on money, walks. His car, an old silver Nissan van, has sat unused since it failed last year's emission test. He hasn't got money to fix it. Surviving on a Pell Grant and disability payments, William lives sparingly but is still sometimes short on the rent. His apartment complex has changed management, and the new policies include strict penalties for late payments. This morning, he overslept and is late for school, so he needs to borrow his friend's bright green Discount Cab. He drives to geology class, ignoring calls from the dispatcher, the heel and palm of his fingerless hand guiding the black steering wheel.

ON A SEPTEMBER EVENING IN 2005, I was hosting a small fundraiser for the Lost Boys Center in Phoenix, too busy to notice the young Sudanese man sitting quietly beneath a tree in my backyard, his stillness like camouflage. Years later, he would tell me how isolated he felt that night. His English was poor, and experience kept him cautious, emotionally distant. He did not trust people's motives and had told no one his real story. Less than a year later, introduced to William at another Lost Boys event, I extended my hand and was startled by the plastic palm and fingers I touched, brown, shiny, lifeless. Eventually, when this young man began calling me Mom, I felt wary of what I might be obligated to do or to give beyond what I was comfortable with, which, frankly, was not much. If the word *mother* is a mythic invocation of selflessness, I owned plenty of selfishness at that point in my life, along with a slew of rich excuses. What I would come to realize, with some shame over this tense instinct for self-preservation, was how much this young man had to offer my two daughters and me. Not materially—for he had and has next to nothing—but by his loyalty and integrity, and by his exceptional story of survival.

When a stranger walks into one's guarded life, a gift disguised as a potential burden, a gentle rebuke to the narrowest notion of family, then the strengthening of one's capacity to risk generosity, the incremental increase in one's courage, feels like uncreeded theology, like some new faith, love's loftiest ideal made human by a series of small, ordinary acts.

The evening I formally met William and shook his hand, he was with his friend Edward Ashhurst, a filmmaker hoping to make a documentary about William's life. Ed asked for my professional help, and, intrigued by what I might learn about his process, I agreed. He and William began visiting me, and over a period of several weeks we fell into a routine. William would tell his story, Ed and I would listen, and then all three of us would talk over possible strategies for the documentary. At one point, we even flew to Los Angeles to meet a producer who had shown interest. But before long, the project stalled. I became busy teaching and traveling and only saw William from time to time. I had also become aware of some slight, unsettling opposition within myself. As much as William's story of being a child slave haunted me, I was resisting its pull. He had confided terrible things to Ed and me, things he said he had never told anyone; perhaps, I reasoned, the connection I resisted was simply one of bearing witness. Even less comfortable to admit was my fascination with the details and depth of his suffering, again offset by an obdurate reluctance to get too close. Closeness, after all, implies a responsibility that voyeurism doesn't. So for a very long time my relationship with William stalled too, in uneasy territory. For a long time, I held him at arm's length.

TODAY, MORE HUMAN BEINGS suffer enslavement than during the three-and-a-half centuries of the transatlantic slave trade. The International Labour Organization, a United Nations agency focused on labor rights, recently—and some would say conservatively—raised its worldwide estimate of the number of individuals unable to escape various forms of forced labor and trafficking from twelve million to nearly twenty-one million. Africa and the Asia-Pacific region together account for the largest number, close to fifteen million people, but slavery is epidemic around the world and increasing.

In Sudan, slavery is not a new phenomenon. Intertribal slave raids, Sudanese Arabs enslaving southern tribal peoples for personal use and export, and the lucrative nineteenth-century European slave trade all played tragic parts in Sudanese history. But in the twentieth century, during Sudan's two scarcely interrupted civil wars, slave raids by Arab militia became an especially brutal strategy of the north. Murahaleen, white-robed Arabs armed with Kalashnikovs, swept down from the north on horseback, raiding and burning Dinka and Nuer villages, seizing thousands of women and children, decimating southern Sudanese tribes defenseless against modern weaponry and government-supported rape, slavery, and genocide. With the north's population predominantly Muslim, and the tribal peoples of the south mostly either animist or Christian, religious divisions and cultural rifts, along with complex historical, agricultural, and environmental factors, including Chevron's discovery of vast oil reserves in the south in the 1970s and the Sudanese government's introduction of sharia law in 1983, created unfortunate, if not inevitable, conditions for civil war.

After fifty years of war, and six years after the Comprehensive Peace Agreement was signed in 2005, Southern Sudan voted in a historic referendum in January 2011 to secede from Sudan. On July 9, 2011, the Republic of South Sudan, led by President Salva Kiir Mayardit, became the world's newest sovereign nation. Today, the Islamist president of Sudan, Omar al-Bashir, continues to deny the existence of as many as thirty-five thousand South Sudanese slaves who remain in his country, and refuses to cooperate with South Sudanese government representatives who want to restore these people to their tribal homes.

Of the thousands of Dinka and Nuer men, women, and children captured in Sudan's murahaleen raids, few have escaped to tell their story.

William Mawwin did break free, and his story begins with

his ancestors, generations before his birth, among the Dinka of southern Sudan.

Manyuol Mawein is the tallest of men, an eight-foot giant. He is also the wealthiest, a tribal chief who owns a vast herd of cattle, thousands, like stars, past counting. He has fifty wives, cattle for fifty more. He has dozens of sons and daughters. During the dry season cattle camp, his family lives in conical mud-walled homes with thatched roofs in his village while Manyuol, with the other men and boys, herds cattle in rich savanna grassland. He sleeps close to his cattle at night. They are his spirit connection to Nhialic, to God, who breathes and moves in all living things. Like all Dinka men, Manyuol is naked but for an elaborately beaded corset signifying status, his readiness for another marriage. His skin and face are coated with a ghostly white ash made from cattle dung fires. His hair, dyed with cow urine and powdered with ash, is a red-gold color considered to be very beautiful. Manyuol is his father's name, his grandfather's name, the name of nine male generations before him and unnumbered generations after him. His bull name is Mawein, after the rare brown-and-white color of his chosen bull, his song ox. He composes songs in praise of Mawein, strongest and noblest of all his bulls, caresses the beast's twin curving horns and his belly, and brushes him clean each day with ash. Mawein's high, white crescent horns, black tassels swaying from their tips, pierce new stars in the sky as he walks. Raising his arms high, Manyuol imitates the curving horns of Mawein as he sings the beauty and number of his cattle, the longevity of his people, the beneficent spirit of Nhialic, of God.

MANYUOL MAWEIN WAS BORN on February 19, 1979, in an army hospital in southern Sudan, the third of six children. His birth name connected him to nine or more generations of Dinka men. As the largest ethnic group in southern Sudan, the Dinka live from the Bahr al-Ghazal region of the Nile basin to Upper Nile and are a pastoral people, cattle herders during the dry season, which begins in December, and cultivators of peanuts, beans, corn, and millet and other grains during the wet season, which begins in the spring. The tallest people on the continent of Africa, the Dinka often reach seven or more feet in height. While early European explorers called them ghostly giants, or gentle giants, in Upper Nile they call themselves *jieng* and in the Bahr al-Ghazal region, *monyjang*, "the men of men." The Dinka are polygamous, though many men have only one wife. A woman can marry the ghost of a male who died in infancy, one of his live relatives standing in for the dead man, and many "ghost fathers" exist among Dinka people. Because of the early influence of British missionaries, many Dinka have converted to Christianity from animist belief. Dressing in cheap, imported Western clothes or the loose-fitting Arab *djellaba* has largely replaced such traditional practices as wearing beaded corsets or whitening the naked body with ash from cow dung fires, a form of decoration that also protects against malarial mosquitoes and tsetse flies.

In 1982, on the cusp of what would become the second Sudanese civil war, two-year-old Manyuol was critically burned in a home cooking-fire accident, an incident that his family, even today, is uncomfortable talking about. William guesses they feel guilty, particularly his mother, and he knows that among Dinka people, whatever is bad about the past is carefully kept in the past. To discuss or dwell on unhappy memories is impolite, even inappropriate. Because of this, though he still bears scars from this accident on his side and back, William understands that he may never learn the details of what happened to him that day. What he does know is that following several months' stay in a hospital, he was returned to his parents in the city of Wau. Soon after, his grandmother, wanting to protect him from the coming

violence, walked seven days from her village of Ajok to bring
Manyuol to live with her. Because of his injuries and young age,
he was the most vulnerable of her grandchildren. He would be
safer in Ajok, with her, than in the city.

*My first memory is walking with Joc, my grandmother, down to
the river to get water. A fisherman gave me my first fish to bring
home. I used to love to walk, talk, and lie down next to my grandmother. She would always make sure I ate first. I never felt she
was a grandmother; she was just like a mother to me. With her, I
had a joyful life. I love my grandmother a lot. I think of her every
day, and know I can never have that life with her again.*

UNABLE TO PAY HIS BILLS, William dropped out of community college classes to take a job as a night security guard at a
bank in Phoenix. Hearing this from his friend Ed, I worried
that William would plummet between the economic cracks,
his hope for an education sacrificed in the monotonous struggle for survival. One morning, before dawn, I was wakened
from a sound sleep by a "voice"—one of the strangest things
I have ever experienced, and nearly impossible to describe—
but this voice was a command, coming from me, yet not "me,"
its directive simple: I *must* pay for William's schooling, for his
tuition and books. Whatever its source, this voice would not
be ignored. Calling William that day, I got to the point. Find
out how much your tuition and books will cost next semester,
and let me know. You need to go back to school, you need to
get your degree. Scarcely believing this wild turn of fortune,
William quit his job, registered for classes, and, with his tuition
and books paid for, would never miss another semester of college. Up to that point, with each low-wage job, he had tried
to set aside money for one or two classes at the community
college, starting with the ESL (English as a second language)

series. At his airport job, when he had asked for a work schedule to accommodate his class times, he was fired. Each month had become an uphill struggle to pay bills. Somehow, William's life in America had turned into a futile exercise, his dreams trumped by poverty.

As for me, obeying that voice was one of the most irrational, least practical, and finest things I have ever done in my life.

Soon afterward, William began calling me Mom. I found it impossible to reciprocate, to call him Son. It felt false, ill fitting. And when he casually mentioned that I might write his story one day, I was politely evasive. Skittish. But this past spring, in a kind of parallel experience to "the voice," I instinctively, though less mystically, came to feel that the time had come to tell his story. So for three straight weeks, William came to my home to be interviewed. Every afternoon we sat in my back guest room, blinds drawn, the dimness offering a kind of sedative twilight I hoped would help him feel safe. I sat across from him on a small white couch, trying not to feel like some impostoring journalist/psychologist as I asked questions and rapidly wrote down each word of every answer. Hours passed with William stretched out in a deep white chair, talking. His chair, my couch, white and solid in the semidarkness, hardly anchored us. Remembering details of his capture and enslavement, he would sometimes break down and cry, something he tries never to do. Still, each time he left my house he was lighter of step, cheerful, as if, in the neutral sanctuary of that back room, he had literally left more baggage behind.

To get to my house each day, William borrowed his friend's taxicab; occasionally during our sessions, he had to answer a phone call, his speech switching rapidly from English to Arabic to Dinka, depending on the caller. He kept these exchanges short or, increasingly often, turned off his phone. Together, we let go of the present and moved backward in time; we began with that winter morning when a boy's childhood, William's, changed irrevocably.

Simple intimacy sprang up between us during these afternoons. At some indeterminate moment, sitting across from him in that shadowy room as he talked, entrusting me with terrible and sometimes pleasant memories, I began to find it natural, a matter of pride as much as affection, to call him my son.

They teach you to suffer. Put a huge fear in your heart. The day you got captured is the day you start your job.

On a bright winter morning in February 1985, six-year-old Manyuol accompanies one of his uncles to the marketplace. Hearing gunshots, Manyuol imagines that men must be hunting close by. Two days later, again in the company of his uncle, the boy stares as men wearing long white robes and white headpieces gallop recklessly into the marketplace on horseback. Murahaleen. They seize cattle, children, women, blankets, clothes, mosquito netting, winter supplies. Dust is everywhere, confusion, gunshots, terrified screams. His uncle is shouting, trying to reach Manyuol, but the boy stands very still, hypnotized by all the noise, the excitement, the horses. He has never seen a horse, wants to touch one. When a man is shot in front of him, he thinks the figure lying in the reddening dirt is going to wake up. Suddenly, one of the white-robed men grabs Manyuol and throws him hard across a horse's back, behind the saddle, tying his arms and legs with rope. Manyuol is one of seventy Dinka boys, girls, and women captured that winter morning by Arab militia. Half will perish before reaching the end of a fifteen-day forced walk; those who survive will be sold, of less worth than cattle, into slavery.

As William recalled that forced walk, his voice was flat, expressionless. Then it broke, and he stopped to cry.

Sometimes what William relates is remembered in the second person, the "you" providing safe distance, a buffer from overwhelming emotions. When he speaks, his tenses frequently blur. Past and present overlap. Time as a straightforward concept dissolves. William's accent is heavy; his diction and syntax are unique, cobbled from hybrid, self-taught languages. At times, he uses clinical phrases culled from sociology or psychology classes; often, his grammar is incorrect, his sentences confusing. (In this essay, I have lightly edited some of William's phrasing for clarity while preserving his meaning as well as his style of speech and transitions from past to present.)

Jotting everything down, I slowly came to realize that there is no proper tense for trauma, no perfect grammar for pain. And when he used the word *skip* for escape, I thought how strange a contradiction that was, using a word most of us associate with play to describe running from captivity. I was jarred each time I heard William, with not a trace of irony, refer to the Arab man who had held him captive as *Master*.

First they shot all the boys and girls who couldn't walk anymore, the four- and five-year-olds. One soldier ties a little boy to a tree, telling us, "If you can't walk anymore, this will happen to you." He shoots the boy, takes a metal rod from the fire, shoves it up the boy's anus. There was a party that night, the boy still hanging dead from the tree.

Another guy stood in front of all of the kids with an AK-47, ordered them to shut their eyes. "If you open your eyes, a bullet will hit you or you will have to shoot another kid." So you close your eyes. He fires off the gun in front of you; it might or might not hit you. You jump like a bullet. One little boy is crying, "Mom, Mom, help me," but the mother is tied, bound hands to ankles with a rope.

A young Arab guy with a mustache—he wore a white head

scarf, carried a white rope—he grabbed this little girl, started laughing when she tried to push him away. He dragged her behind a tree, tore off her clothes; we were all watching. Her brother, naked, my age, tied up like us, jumped to his feet, started yelling at the man to to leave his sister alone. No one said anything. The Arab guy turned, shot the boy three times in the chest. Put holes in his chest. The mother was crying, crying. They taped her mouth shut, and the next day, shot her in the mouth. Her baby kept trying to get milk from the dead mother.

That little boy lay right next to me. He was my age. His foot was jerking, blood was coming out of his mouth and nose, he turned his head and smiled straight into my eyes, died. That little boy is the one person I would never, never, never forget in my life. He is a hero to me.

WHAT DID THEY GIVE YOU TO EAT?

Rice with insects in it. They forced you to eat it. It gave you diarrhea.

CAN YOU DESCRIBE THE WALK?

We walked at night because it was cooler for the cattle, and because we couldn't tell where we were going. You walk and walk, you get so tired, don't know where you are.

DID YOU KNOW ANY OF THE WOMEN OR OTHER CHILDREN?

Yes. One of the kids was a cousin of mine; he's still in captivity today.

HOW DID THEY MAKE ALL OF YOU WALK?

In a straight line, holding a rope, two people tied together. Everyone is naked, you have to sleep on cold ground. If you need to pee, you ask, then everyone has to get up with you. At night you can't see anything—you might step on a snake, a scorpion, get bitten and die. It happened.

One morning, this three- or four-year-old boy, too little to be tied up with the older kids, wakes up cold, tries to go nearer to the fire everyone is sleeping around, gets shot.

If you are weak, you die. If you smile, you die.

Another boy is shot dead because he is sick, then his mother and sister are killed with a machete, because they are weeping.

If you show emotion, you die.

I kept thinking about my grandmother, thinking my grandmother will come and save me. Somehow she will save me.

You have to save yourself.

By the time we reach Babanusa [a town in western Sudan], maybe thirty kids are alive. Half died or were left, sick, by the road, with no food or water.

DO YOU EVER DREAM ABOUT IT?

Every night until I was seventeen. I still dream sometimes about it.

There was one little girl, only four or five years old, wearing a long blue skirt. They ripped off her skirt, hung it on a tree. She got raped by a lot of men. Afterward she said, "When I die, will you tell my father?" She walked for three days after that, naked, bleeding, until she died, until she was free.

I keep seeing that blue skirt.

At the slave market everyone is naked, sitting on the ground. They test you, look you over. They divide you—women, children, young ladies. If you are related, they separate you. They count you, one by one. Now your name, your identity, is an Arabic number: six women, thirty kids, some girls. The Arab women do the selecting. They are looking for slaves to cook, to clean, do laundry, iron. The older kids are taken first, the eight- to eleven-year olds. Then seven to five. Nobody takes children under five unless that child is with a woman or one of the women takes the child to raise as a slave. Girls are valuable for sex. By the age of fifteen or sixteen, a girl will have two or three children by her slave owners, and she will raise them, like her, to be slaves.

This Arab family bought seven of us, five boys and two girls. I ended up with the old man, my master. His name was Ahmed Sulaman Jubar. He picked me because I spoke a little Arabic. To speak Arabic made you more valuable. He named me Ali, and I had to recite from the Koran, pray five times a day with him. I had to call him Dad, his wife Mom. Their children, I was told, were my brothers and sisters.

We walked one-and-a-half days more. Then with the old man, two of his sons, and a Dinka woman with her daughter, I walked four days more with all the cattle. Everyone spoke Arabic. I didn't understand anything. When we got to a temporary house, I ate real food, drank milk. I still don't know what's going on. I sit under a tree, fall asleep there. Next day, I'm still there. Two days later, I got my first order—go with one of the master's sons, take the sheep and goats to get water.

I never sit down to rest until I skip five years later.

You're beaten, slapped, you don't understand the language, you have to memorize what they say. For two months they tie your hands and feet every night, you sleep on the ground with the cattle. There is nowhere to go. After that, I got picked to take care of the old man. My duties: be his nurse, companion, walk him to the mosque for prayers. His wife stayed in Babanusa with the children and grandchildren. My master liked staying in the country with his cattle and sheep. When his wife would visit, she was terrible, mean like hell, really, really mean. When she comes, it is the worst time for everybody. She sits there cooking her coffee all day, complaining, yelling, crying.

In the morning I cook, bring his tea, black tea with milk, his bread. I cook the bread, too. I fold his bed. I cook his lunch, usually chicken. I do his laundry, using a bucket with water and soap. Lay his clothes in the sun to dry. Master would pray five times a day, he was really into the Koran. Then I start going to cattle camp, rotating with his youngest son, three months younger than me, the son he loved more than anything. When this son was around, I had to leave, go to cattle camp, get yelled at, beaten. One time, when I lost one of the cows, Ahmad, the fourth son, stabbed me, told me find the cow or he will kill me. After I find it, he still slaps me, beats me, gets really rough.

For four years, I didn't go anywhere. Master told me: Your parents did not want you, now I'm taking care of you. All this is going to be yours one day. I will find you a wife. These are your brothers. You are part of our family. This will be your special cow. So you feel motivated, work very hard. But it is psychological manipulation. Sweet talk. Mind control.

When I was ten, Master took me with him to Babanusa for the first time. It was Ramadan, so we went to buy stuff and to sell cows, goats, sheep. The city was so beautiful! Master had this beautiful house, a city house. We live in it four days, the four most beautiful days ever. I start asking him, "Why do we live in the jungle with cows, why can't we live here, in the city?" Why, I ask myself, am I living tied up, with rules? In Babanusa, Master buys me cookies. I had never tasted sweets before. I see cars everywhere, and everywhere I see people looking like me, Dinka people, working for themselves. Before, I thought I was my master's son or maybe his grandson, but when I see all of these people in the city, especially Dinka people, I get my first idea to skip. Back at camp, my dream becomes Babanusa. I start thinking how I will skip. I behave well so Master will take me with him back to the city. I dedicate myself to him, be loyal to him. Become his best slave so he will trust me.

AHMED JUBAR TAKES THE BOY, Ali, to the market in Babanusa for a second time, to sell cattle and buy supplies. On a third trip, Ali is made to go with Ahmed's fourth son, Ahmad, the one who had once stabbed and beaten him for losing a cow. Ali works all day, washing and ironing mountains of clothes, taking care of Ahmad's four children, staying awake all night to watch the cattle, always terrified Ahmad will kill him. Still, he has an extra day in Babanusa with Ahmad and his family, and, at a tea stall, meets an older boy who tells him about an even bigger city, El Obeid. "Babanusa is nothing!" the boy says.

Six months later, Ali, now eleven, returns to the tea stall to look for that same boy, but instead meets Chol, a twenty-nine-year-old Dinka truck driver. This time, Ali is in Babanusa with three other slave kids he met in cattle camp. These other boys are fifteen, thirteen, and twelve, all older than Ali. After meeting Chol, the four of them talk about how they might escape captivity on their next trip into the city.

On Ali's fifth trip, he walks into Babanusa with the other three boys. They find Chol. He buys them food, lets them keep the money they've just made from selling cow's milk. When Ali says he wants to go to El Obeid, Chol answers, "I can get a job for you there, but you have to pay me. I have four trucks leaving tonight with cattle and peanuts. I can take you and your three friends." Ali gives Chol his milk money, makes sure the other boys have a way out, too. They are all runaway slaves now; anybody who gets caught will be beaten, get a foot chopped off, or be killed. If Ali skips on his own, he knows the other boys will be blamed, punished, possibly killed. He decides he can only leave if he helps them escape too, so he invents a story, telling the boys he will wait in Babanusa overnight, watching the cows, while they go in trucks to other cities to buy more cows and bring them back the next day. Believing him, two of the boys go off in one of Chol's trucks, and the third goes by himself in a different truck to another city. Like Ali, they have given Chol their money. After they are safely gone, Ali waits until dark to leave with Chol. The boy is shaky, scared. He can't relax until they reach El Obeid the next afternoon.

I am alive today because of that truck driver. He saved my life trafficking me, taking my money, selling me to another master. There is no help given for free. I was a transaction.

CHOL DRIVES TO EL OBEID, the capital of North Kordofan State, and at four the next afternoon delivers Ali to a Muslim family. Ali is astonished to see Chol sitting down and eating with the man of the house, laughing, cussing, using the same plates, drinking from the same cups. The wife brings Ali food, examines him, touches him, seems happy he is there.

He will work seven months for this family and never be paid. Sharing a room with another Dinka slave, a seventeen-year-old boy called Deng, Ali will find life in El Obeid worse than cattle camp, where at least he could be outdoors, could hunt, fish, and drink cow's milk. Here, inside this house, there is no escape. He works all the time. The first two months, he has to watch the family's children, walk them to and from school, do all the washing and ironing. After that, he is made to do everything, all the cleaning, and gets beaten if something is not done right. But a happy respite, even a new name, comes when he meets Father Tarticchio.

Sometimes I walk past this church. I see kids running in a field nearby, falling, shouting, laughing, playing with a ball. I watch them. One day, a priest with gray hair and a white mustache comes up to me. His name, he says, is Father Tarticchio. He speaks Arabic and wears a white robe, a red hat, Sudanese slippers, and uses a stick to walk. I find out that he helps all the street kids, gives them clothing, feeds them, helps them go to school. When he drives his little white car, some kind of Italian jeep, everybody waves at him. He's well loved in El Obeid. The day he gives me a green T-shirt with a picture of Bishop Daniel Comboni on it, I start wearing it all the time. [Saint Daniel Comboni was a missionary credited with numerous conversions in Africa in the nineteenth century.] *I start going to Bible study at the church because it is so peaceful. One Sunday, Father Tarticchio baptizes me, gives me a new, Christian name,* William. *After William Wallace, he says. Who's that? A Scottish warrior, also called Braveheart.*

I start going on Sundays to Father Tarticchio's church. I think the Communion wafer is food, bread, so every Sunday I go up there and eat it. The explanation of what it is doesn't make sense to me, but I go up there to be fed. In church, it is peaceful. Nobody slaps you, nobody hurts you, and there's free food. As a kid, you don't know anything, you go for the food, the clothes, a bathroom.

I want to play with the kids on the field, but don't know how. Father Tarticchio makes me a goalkeeper, teaches me how. After that, I sneak out of the house whenever I can to play soccer with the other kids. That was the most beautiful thing ever, playing soccer, being a kid.

CHOL STOPS BY THE HOUSE after four months. When Ali, now baptized William, tells him he has not been paid for any of his work, Chol answers, that's because you have to pay me back for the next two years, my price for getting you out. Either that or I will return you to your master, and he can punish you, kill you, for running away. After Chol leaves, William gets beaten more; now he has to ask permission to leave the house. Deng tells him Chol has been stealing William's "earned" money all along, and starts to talk about Khartoum, a bigger city than El Obeid. With Deng helping him, William plans how he will skip. He agrees to work for Deng's cousin in Khartoum for one month, and then he will be free.

As he did with Ahmed Jubar, William puts on a show of loyalty to the family, works even harder. Before walking the kids to school, he puts on extra clothing, drops it off at the cousin's house. One month later, he tells the wife, "Please, I need to buy some clothes." Trusting him, she gives him money to go shopping.

You're poor. Desperate. You're a slave. You're naive, too, and want to believe what people tell you.

Each person influences you the way he wants, then turns mean. You get used to it. You don't care anymore.

You decide you're not worth anything. You wonder, Who will treat me with honesty and kindness? Who will love me just for who I am?

When you are a street kid, you cry and cry and cry and reach a point where you feel nothing anymore. That protects you. You force yourself to have relations with that person who is bad to you.

Emotionless. Forgetting.

When you have no family to care for you, you become a person who has already given up on his life, with nothing to lose. When you have nobody, people know it, and they beat you. If you have a family, you are protected.

And in Khartoum, everybody can tell if you are Nubian, Dinka, Nuer. They take advantage of you, are cruel because you are poor.

Still, God helps you.

WILLIAM DROPS HIS CHARGES OFF at school and keeps going. When the family realizes he has run off with the money they gave him, they go looking for him. He hides at Deng's cousin's place a few days, until he and the cousin take the bus together to Khartoum, a twelve-hour ride. In Khartoum, the national capital, William sees a lot of other Dinka people standing around. He thinks the marketplace is huge, beautiful. The next day, he starts working for Deng's cousin, selling cups of cold drinking water at the market. After two months, he is still selling cups of water, and Deng's cousin is taking half of his money. Since this is not fair, not the agreement, William leaves. The cousin finds William trying to sell water on his own, beats him up, takes his money, threatens to kill him. William is learning a pattern with people—they act nice at first, then control you with fear and beatings. He starts over, tries hustling for money at the marketplace. Three days later, the cousin finds him, beats and robs him again. So he discovers a different marketplace in the city, and at night he sleeps on church rooftops. He spends his days hanging around warehouses, waiting for work loading trucks. Sometimes he goes door to door offering to wash clothes, clean houses. Work is all he has, a refuge. He takes pride in how well he works, does extra work for free. Now thirteen, William will live like this for the next five years.

Life on the street has different values. There is no emotion. Work becomes a silent language, and the kid who beats me up today might be my friend tomorrow.

AKEC, ANOTHER STREET KID, becomes William's first real friend. Hot tempered but loyal, Akec is quick to defend William in fights. One morning, they are riding a public bus together when government soldiers climb aboard and seize all the boys. They find seven boys, including William and Akec, and later release two who are too young. The soldiers in Khartoum are looking for street kids sixteen or seventeen and up, to put into military training and then send south to fight their own people. William and Akec are made to get on a bus with the other three boys and are driven toward a training camp hours away. When the bus stops somewhere en route, all the boys jump out and start running. Akec and William hide in a nearby soccer stadium until the soldiers give up looking for them. Catching a public bus back to Khartoum, they are too frightened to go outside for three days, and stop going to the city's center. They find work with Manyon, an older Dinka man. Sleeping outside his house, they sell things, do construction work, whatever he finds for them to do. They work for Manyon two years before they discover he is cheating them, giving them less than half of the money they have earned. When he figures out they know, Manyon calls the police and accuses Akec and William of stealing from him. The police arrest the boys. Every day in prison, freezing water is thrown on them, and they are beaten with switches. There is no court date, no trial. Seven days later, they are driven to a prison farm several hours outside Khartoum.

At the prison farm, you work sixteen hours a day, sleep in this little hut. Ninety percent of prison-farm workers are southern Sudanese, Dinka, some Nubians. Men, women, children, working on this huge, huge farm the size of a city, growing food for Khartoum.

You wake at 3:00 a.m., have to put this lightbulb on your head so you can see. By 4:00 a.m., you're packing in the dark, loading trucks with vegetables, tomatoes, okra, corn. Every other week, somebody dies from a snakebite. If you die there, people in prison bury you. By 5:00 or 6:00 a.m., the trucks leave for the market. Seven days a week, you are in bed by 8:00 p.m., up working at 3:00 a.m.

After two months we get free, but have no money. We stay working at the farm an extra week to pay for a bus ride to Khartoum. Instead, we decide to keep the money we've earned and ride in the farm truck to the city. At the marketplace, we have to unload the truck, wait around all day, then load the truck back up again before we are really free.

BUT MISFORTUNE DOGS THE BOYS. On their first day of freedom, they happen upon a spot where a southern Sudanese man has just run off after killing someone. Akec and William are apprehended and accused of the murder. Sitting in shackles in yet another jail, interrogated, beaten, lashed every night, William and his friend won't be released until seven months later, when the real murderer is found and arrested. It is May 1997 when they get out, and soon the boys find work with a Dinka man named Wael. They sell used clothes in the market, and Wael pays them and gives them food. He is like a father to them. William remembers Wael as the first person since he was captured to sit down with him and eat off the same plate.

The one nice thing that happens to you when you are in prison is you get to talk all day long about what you will do when you get out. Who you will be. When I get married, you say, or when I get a job, or what I will eat when I get out, when I become a person. When you have a dream life, a second life, you can forget you're in prison. Then, when you get free of being accused of killing someone, it becomes like the toughest thing ever. You're so happy when you get out, have the freedom to start your dream life. The same work you did in prison, you get paid to do. But when Wael gets killed in a car accident, Akec says let's get out of this city, it's bad luck for us. He leaves for Port Sudan. I decide to stay. At least I know where I am, it's familiar.

But after Akec leaves me, I live in a world of darkness.

Toward the end of 1997, it seems like everybody is going to Egypt. I meet Majok. He asks me to help him load things onto a truck, I start helping him, we talk. I am his only Dinka worker, but my Dinka is terrible, since I mostly learned it from Akec.

I don't trust Majok. I am afraid, don't want to tell him my story. After three weeks, he finds me in the market and says, "Okay, Okay, just work with me, stay here, you'll get paid."

"I've worked for many, many people, and all I got was jail," I tell him. I don't want his help. Then Majok's wife tells me her husband's story, convinces me he's a good guy. I go back to working for him.

One day I tell Majok I want to go to Egypt.

"Egypt? I can get you fake papers to go to Egypt. What do you want to do in Egypt?"

"Open my own store, sit in front of it, sell things. I'm tired of the streets. I want a peaceful life."

"I have a store, let me show it to you. I have a house, a family, a store."

"You're rich," I say.

Majok brings me to his home to live, but I am not comfortable in his nice house. Why? I have no trust in anybody anymore. I cut the leather inside my shoe, make a pocket, keep my money there. A street kid trick, your money lives in your shoe. At night I hide my money in a condensed-milk can, bury it in a hole I've dug in the ground, a place people walk by every day, so they won't suspect. I make money selling water, washing clothes, ironing clothes, cleaning, working at the airport baggage claim, anything.

Finally, I can give Majok one thousand Sudanese pounds, that's maybe around two hundred dollars, for a fake passport. I am crying when I give him that money. Later, I will find out he overcharged me. Cheated me.

"Don't tell anybody you have a passport, don't tell anybody you are leaving for Egypt," he says.

I am starting to feel closer to Majok when he tells me, "Okay, you leave tomorrow, this guy is ready to take you. You'll ride in his car between Khartoum and Shendi [a Nile River town northeast of Khartoum]. *Tell everybody you work for me."*

In Shendi, with no ticket, I jump on a train to Wadi Halfa [a town on a large lake that straddles the Egypt-Sudan border]. *I have no money for food, no place to sleep—I'm just waiting to get on the boat to Egypt. Then I get arrested for not having a train ticket. I don't get released until the boat has already left.*

I end up staying in Wadi Halfa, hustling to make money for a boat ticket. Every Friday night, the boat leaves for Aswân [in Egypt], *so after six days, I go to the place I was supposed to meet this guy at. When I find him, he tells me, "The boat leaves at 5:00 p.m. Meet me tomorrow at 4:00 p.m., not 4:01, not 4:05."*

I am there at 3:40.

"Where's the money?" he asks. He takes my money and smuggles me inside this huge plastic container on the dock. I'm in that container for two hours. It's so hot, I can't breathe, I'm sweating. Finally, somebody pushes the container onto the boat; I have to wait one more hour until I hear the boat whistle and can open the container and climb out.

After the boat arrives in Aswân, I give the police guy at immigration my passport and what's left of my money. He takes the money, nods, stamps the passport. "Okay, go ahead."

I ride the train to Cairo, with maybe five or six hundred other Sudanese guys. It takes twelve hours.

February 22, 1998. I am nineteen, finally in Cairo. It's the most beautiful city, crowded. Now I can start my own business, my big dream fulfilled. But where to stay? I know nobody, have no money. What food do I eat?

I find a Catholic church where all the Sudanese go. I am given food and an empty room in exchange for working in the church. It's hard to find work, so the church helps people. I stay there two months until I get a job working in the back of a shoe store. Three months later, I get fired because I don't have a visa.

AFTER WILLIAM IS FIRED from the shoe store for not having a visa—a visa costs money—he goes to the UN office in Cairo

and has someone help him fill out an application for a UN iden-
tification badge. If he is stopped by police, at least he will have
this. Over the next several months, he hustles for money just
as he did in Khartoum, until the local Catholic church finds
him a second job, this one at a factory that makes car batter-
ies, rubber tires, plastics. He works there one month before he
decides he wants to work in the salt mines, digging salt with
some of his friends. He goes into the factory to quit, but his
boss says he can't leave until he gets paid for that day's work.
He takes William to a machine he has never operated before, a
machine that wraps hot plastic onto giant rolls. When William
objects, saying he doesn't know how to operate the machine,
the boss replies, "Figure it out," and walks off. It is August 31,
1999. Hanging on the wall in front of him, used to measure
worker output every thirty minutes and to monitor ten-minute
breaks every two hours for the workers, is a large black-and-
white factory clock. Because of that clock, William will never
forget the time: 12:04 p.m.

Part of my body is still there, in Egypt.

MUCH OF WHAT WILLIAM TOLD ME during those three weeks,
sitting in the shadowy back room of my house, was painful for
him to remember. But aside from the account of his capture by
the Murahaleen, this was the worst of our sessions. His voice
dropped as the details of the factory accident emerged in a
short, scarcely audible rush.

As William attempts to "figure out" how the machine works,
its giant roller snags his right arm and yanks it in. Instinctively,
he uses his left hand to try to pull it back out.

Two Sudanese workers run over, stop the machine, and free
his mangled right arm and left hand from the machine. They
take him to a hospital, but William is not an Egyptian citizen.

He is illegal, illegally employed, so no one wants to treat him. His right arm is crushed to a bloody pulp. The fingers on his left hand are gone. (Today, William still won't eat meat, not for moral reasons, but because meat, cooked or uncooked, reminds him of how the flesh of his arm and hand looked that day.) The Sudanese coworkers spend four hours at the hospital, trying to locate a private doctor willing to perform at-home surgery. Then William becomes frightened. He has heard stories, since verified, of Egyptians killing illegals and selling their organs for profit, so he decides against any surgery outside a hospital. One of the Sudanese takes William's ID badge to the UN office, tells them what happened. Around 5:00 p.m., someone from the UN shows up and takes William to a hospital. In surgery that night, the anesthetic doesn't work. He can see and feel everything. Five days later, the pain is still so terrible, he is taken to another hospital, run by Coptic Christians, for additional surgery, then to a house somewhere in Cairo to recover. At the second hospital, he is given a get-well card, a Bible in Arabic, and a crucifix he will wear every day for years.

The factory owner is hunting for William, wanting to get rid of him as a potential witness.

Because of his accident, UN officials have learned that other illegal Sudanese workers are employed at the factory as well, and they plan to investigate. To avert this, the owner fires all of his Sudanese workers two days after William's accident. The UN never follows up, never investigates employment conditions or the factory owner, so today, apparently no record exists of William's accident or of the illegal workers. Meanwhile, with his life still in danger, William is moved to a UN safe house with a security guard posted outside the door.

Now the UN officials in Cairo begin looking for ways to get William quickly out of Egypt. They try relocating him to Norway, then Denmark, then Belgium, but in all three countries, the requisite paperwork takes a minimum of thirty days. At the US Embassy, things move far faster, and within two days William is on a TWA flight out of Cairo with a few items of clothing, his refugee bag, and some doctor's papers. During the flight, his arm begins hemorrhaging; he begins to go into shock. The plane makes an emergency landing in Amsterdam, where he will spend the next twenty-eight days in a hospital.

Finally, on January 16, 2000, he is flown to New York City. William is twenty years old.

I am in this big hotel, in a room that looks down on a cemetery. My hands are wrapped up, bandaged. I don't speak English. I watch the TV, stand at the window, look down at gravestones, snow. My dream was to have my own shop, sit in front of it, sell things.

Phoenix, Arizona

William arrives at Sky Harbor International Airport at 4:00 p.m. on Friday, February 18, 2000. A caseworker from the Catholic Charities Refugee Resettlement Program is there to meet him. She drives him to an apartment in Phoenix, shows him a refrigerator filled with food, then leaves. William is left alone in the apartment Friday night, Saturday, Saturday night, Sunday, Sunday night. He can't use his bandaged hands to eat or to drink, and the skin graft on his leg has become infected. *I was in so much pain, it was like being a slave, tied up again.* He understands no English, only remembers that during an orientation class in Cairo he had been sternly warned about dangers in America, told never to open the door for any reason, never to speak to strangers, never to stare at anyone. Exhausted, terrified, sick, he is depending for his survival on a woman whose language he doesn't speak, a woman who has disappeared. He doesn't know how to eat most of the food in the refrigerator; it looks too strange to him. When he finds some juice, he drinks that. The caseworker returns on Monday, unlocks the front door, comes in, and finds William lying in bed. Thinking he is sick, she drives him to a doctor. But because William speaks only Arabic and Dinka, no one understands what he is trying to tell them. *I'm so hungry. I'm in pain*. The doctor changes the bandages on his leg, and then the woman takes him to the Refugee Resettlement office. By then, he is shaking all over but can't tell anyone what is wrong. When he sees a Muslim woman coming down the stairs, he speaks to her in Arabic. *Please, tell these people I haven't eaten in four days. My leg is hurting. Please, I need help.*

The woman, a refugee from Iraq, understands, and soon William is fed his first food in days. As they sit in a McDonald's, the caseworker indicates to the Muslim woman, who has volunteered to come with them, that he had plenty of food in his apartment. No, the woman answers, his hands don't work. He can't eat. She then feeds him french fries with her fingers, and it is not lost on William that the first person to understand him in his new home, the first person to give him what he needs—nourishment—is a Muslim.

Most of the other Sudanese guys came here as Lost Boys, but there is a huge difference between the Lost Boys and me. I was captured when I was six, was a slave, then a street kid. The Lost Boys walked from the jungle to a refugee camp in Kenya, then came to American cities. Our experiences are not the same. It's really sad—many of them have had trouble, have died in car accidents, are in prison or living on the street, homeless.

WILLIAM IS MOVED into another apartment in a plain but neatly kept area of Phoenix. Arcadia Palms is a glaringly white two-story apartment complex, its muddy aqua trim softened by the city's ubiquitous palm trees and an occasional splash of fuchsia bougainvillea. The complex is filled with refugees, mostly Sudanese. William has two roommates, Malak from the Democratic Republic of the Congo, and Gurang from Sudan. Malak picks a fight with Gurang, moves out, and soon after is relocated to Nebraska. William will live in that apartment for three years, eventually with five Sudanese roommates, all six young men sharing a one-bedroom apartment that rents for $515 a month. There is a lot of drinking and weed, and three of his roommates get into trouble with the law.

Six months after his arrival in Phoenix, William meets Jim, another person who will change his life.

In October 2000, I meet a guy named Achile, the education coordinator for ESL at Catholic Social Services. Achile introduces me to this older gentleman in his fifties or sixties named Jim. Jim had two big trucks, mostly he drove this big Ford diesel pickup. The first time he picked me up at my apartment, he is talking, talking, talking to me. I don't know what he is saying. He took me to Coco's on Forty-Sixth and Thomas for lunch. He orders steak and spinach for himself, fish for me, with blueberries and cake for dessert. He sat and ate, then drove me to the library down the road. He got me a library card and checked out some children's books. He sat with me in the library until 2:00 p.m., teaching me to read from those children's books. The next day, Jim brought some ESL papers to my apartment, then we went to another restaurant on Indian School and Thirty-Second Street. We sat in a far corner and, again, he ordered me fish. We became friends after that second time in the restaurant. For three months, Jim came to my apartment three times a week and drove me to the library to teach me English.

The last time Jim took me out to eat, we went to a really nice fish place on Fortieth and Campbell. I remember he was drinking water, then started choking, coughing a lot. I worried maybe he was sick.

That was the last time I ever saw Jim. After he dropped me back at my apartment, he said something I didn't understand, and when he didn't show up the next time, I tried to find him by calling Achile. Achile told me Jim had moved to New York. "When I come back from my hiking trip next week, I'll give you his phone number."

Four days later, I learned Achile was dead from a fall.

The world became a dark place.

Jim did so much for me. I couldn't tell him. Can you imagine? Three times a week for three months to teach you, to feed you for free, and you don't speak English, so you can't tell him how you feel?

If Jim is alive, I'd take him to the same restaurants, sit in the same places. "What did you tell me that day? I didn't understand you then, but now I can tell you what I am feeling." It's a silent talk I have over and over in my heart, but I can't ever tell him. I can't look in his eyes, at his face. I can't ever tell him.

Jim is the reason I learned English. I want one day to meet him, to show him: This is my associate's degree, my bachelor's degree. Thank you.

I can't go to that library anymore, where we used to sit with the children's books.

DURING ONE INTERVIEW SESSION, I asked William what jobs he'd had since coming to Arizona. Stoically, he ticked them off: delivering pizza for Papa John's and Domino's, making gum in a candy factory, working in a parking booth at the airport, working as a night security guard in a bank downtown. Every time he applied for a new job, he would be questioned about his disability, asked how could he do the work. "Don't let my arms intimidate you," he would answer. "Give me two days, and if it doesn't work out, tell me. I will respect your opinion." Since his escape from slavery, since his factory accident, William has only wanted one thing: independence.

In the long run, no matter what, I have to do things for myself. I changed my own tire when my car broke down. Nothing is hard when you put your mind into it. Just focus, relax your mind, and you will do it. It is fear that gets you hurt.

WILLIAM HAS A CAR AND A JOB, and things are almost peaceful for him when he meets an eighteen-year-old American girl who likes hanging around the Sudanese refugee guys; when William meets her, he offers to help with some family problems she is having. Soon, she is calling a lot, asking for rides here and there. As he told me about her, I hesitated to press for details. "After a while, we got together," he simply said. He had been naive, he added, to have gotten involved, though he still carried a photo of her in his wallet.

I wore black every day to show I was dead but still walking around. I started dressing like this in Africa, after I got out of captivity. Wearing white meant a peaceful day, a better day for me. If I wore black and white, mixed, that meant anything could happen, good or bad. I dressed almost always in black, until the day I became a father.

ON THE LAST DAY OF SEPTEMBER 2003, William is in school, taking an ESL class. A security guard comes in to get him, and he drives to Arrowhead Hospital. He stays all that night and two days more. On October 2, at 1:45 a.m., William's daughter is born by C-section, and William is there to cut the umbilical cord. Afterward, he goes outside the building, sits down, and cries. He told me that by the time he went back inside the hospital, his whole perspective on life had changed.

William and his girlfriend give the baby a Dinka name, Achol.

Up to then, I told people what they wanted to hear. Kept to myself. I was like a ghost, empty, living day by day. I didn't care about my life. Today, I have someone to live for, to say I love you, words you never hear before. When somebody calls you Dad, you feel so proud.

HE STAYS THREE DAYS at the hospital, leaving only once to buy some baby clothes and a car seat. On the fifth day, William drives the baby and his girlfriend to her mother's apartment. When his daughter gets sick and has to go back into the hospital, William quits his job to take care of his new family. He drops out of school. Soon, there are problems with his girlfriend.

He is living in an apartment with five other Sudanese men, saving money for a place of his own, when the court awards him sole custody of his daughter once he is financially stable. In the meantime, his girlfriend's aunt and uncle are to take care of the baby. Although William is allowed to see his daughter whenever he wants, it is still hard for him to let her go.

In my apartment, I have a T-shirt that says Daddy's Girl with Achol's picture on it. I still have the teddy bear I brought to the hospital the day she was born. It stays on her bed in my apartment. Sometimes I sit and hold that teddy bear and try not to think I'm a failure. I tell myself I am a father, and my daughter is the first happiness of my life.

In Dinka, Achol *means "reward after long troubles."*
A joy. A happiness.

In North America, the Sudanese refugee network is extensive and strong, deeply reflective of tribal culture. Through it, lost friends and relatives are located and reunited. In 2005, William attends a large Sudanese gathering in Nashville and meets a young man who knew one of William's brothers, Abey. He says Abey is living in Calgary, Canada. Returning to Phoenix, William calls Abey, and on May 17, 2005, he flies to Calgary with Ed Ashhurst, the filmmaker. Soon after the brothers' reunion, their relatives in Ajok learn that William is still alive, living in America. When he speaks to his father on the phone for the first time, William does not mention the factory accident in Cairo or his disability. He decides to wait until the day his family sees him, and in December 2009 he is given a miraculous gift—the opportunity to return home. He has been tutoring a student in his math class at Scottsdale Community College, and when the student's father hears William's story, he volunteers to pay William's airfare to Sudan for Christmas. William has not seen his family for more than twenty years.

On December 28, 2009, I flew to Wau, then drove to Ajok. I arrived home at 3:00 a.m. I didn't tell anyone I was coming—I didn't believe I was there myself. All the trees, the jungle, everything—look different than you remember. The village is not the village I used to know. People look different, grown up, married, with two or three wives and kids. The people I loved, like my grandmother, were mostly all dead. Still, people came out from everywhere and start crying. My mom had moved from Wau back to Ajok, and when she came outside and saw me, she fell to the ground, went unconscious. All these years she believed I was dead.

The first place I went to visit was my grandmother Joc's grave. She died in 2004. Her house still had my uncle living in it. I went inside to see her old room and slept there my first night. I thought

if I could feel her presence, let her know I'm back, it will complete
my happiness. It was a huge moment for me at first, then empty.
She's not here, not in her room, my grandmother is dead. Maybe,
I think, she'll see me in the spiritual way.

IN JUNE 2010, when charity activist and former NBA basketball
star Manute Bol dies in the United States, his family asks if William will escort Manute's body home for burial. Manute is from
Turalei, a Dinka village not far from William's village of Ajok,
and Manute's father is powerful, well known, "like an emperor
or a king among Dinka people," William explained. The families know one another and are distantly related by marriage. In
Phoenix, after attending a cousin's graduation at Arizona State
University, Manute met William; they talked and played domi-
noes. William has a photo of himself with Manute and one of
Manute's sisters at her wedding. He agrees to escort Manute's
body home to Turalei and attends his funeral. Afterward he
travels to Cairo, then to Khartoum, where he searches for and,
incredibly, locates the family that had owned him as a slave.

The old man, Ahmed Jubar, is dead, but investigating further, William locates Jubar's fourth son, Ahmad, the one who
had stabbed him. William calls Ahmad, says he is in Khartoum and wishes to see the Jubar family again. The two men
meet, sit down together, and immediately Ahmad denies that
William, as Ali, had ever been his family's slave. He had been
a part of their family, well treated. Why had he run away? If
he hadn't run off, then that—here Ahmad indicates William's
arm and hand—would never have happened. William invents
a story to gain Ahmad's trust, saying that one day in Babanusa,
a man had offered him a ride in a car, then taken him away.
He hadn't run away, he had been kidnapped! William says
he is now a college student in America, and Ahmad, initially
incredulous, soon asks for William's help in getting his own

son into an American college. Uneasily reunited, William and Ahmad travel to Babanusa to see the rest of the family. Every member of the Jubar family, including the old man's widow, denies William had ever been beaten or mistreated, had ever been a slave. They insist he had been part of their own family, well cared for, until he made the poor choice to run away, or, as William explains to them, had been kidnapped. After he returns to Phoenix, it takes William a long time to process the Jubars' blatant denial, their collective insistence that he had never been a slave, that he had never been harmed by any one of them.

I wanted to find the old man and forgive him. Without him capturing me, I would not be in America. So a bad thing, being captured, taken from my village, turned to a good thing. I wanted to show that family who I had become, how I had changed my name from Ali to William, how I live in the West now. I wanted them to see the difference between who I was with them—a slave—and who I am today.

In January 2011, William and Ed fly for a third time from Phoenix to Ajok so that William can vote in the referendum on an independent southern Sudan. And in early July, William returns with Ed to celebrate the birth of the Republic of South Sudan. The new Government of South Sudan (GOSS) has extended an invitation to a number of Sudanese college students living in America, William among them, to help host the ceremonies in Juba, the new state's capital. On his first day in Juba, wearing an official GOSS press badge, William drives to the airport to greet and escort UN secretary general Ban Ki-moon; the vice president of Cuba, Esteban Lazo Hernández; and the president of Zimbabwe, the infamous Robert Mugabe. The next day, William returns to the airport to greet Susan

Rice, US ambassador to the United Nations. William refuses to greet or escort Omar al-Bashir, the president of Sudan. At a news conference later that day in the presidential palace, William shakes hands with Salva Kiir Mayardit, the first president of South Sudan. And on July 9, 2011, wearing the red jacket he bought in America just for this occasion, William watches as the black, red, green, and blue South Sudanese flag is raised for the first time. He listens as President Mayardit; Ambassador Rice; the British foreign secretary, William Hague; and many others speak, even al-Bashir. Later, William will say it was the best, happiest day of his life, the day of independence for his new country, the Republic of South Sudan.

In Juba, William is offered a number of promising jobs. Because of his fluency in English and his education—hard won but hardly elite, at least in the United States—he is a valuable asset to a new nation with a 27 percent literacy rate, a 51 percent poverty rate, and a population that is 83 percent rural. The government offers him a job overseeing the building of roads and infrastructure; the UN wants to hire him to assist people with disabilities in South Sudan, and the governor of Wau is interested in having him help disabled schoolchildren. The Sudan People's Liberation Movement (the current ruling political party in South Sudan, headquartered in Juba), along with other political parties in Juba, are also interested in his potential contribution to the fledgling republic. And William is clear about his aspirations to set a new example for a culture that sees no value in disability. He wants to set an example by his education and his refusal to let disability limit him. The job offers are flattering, even tempting, but he turns each one down, explaining that he needs to return to America and earn his college degree before he can help his country in the ways he dreams of. Beyond agricultural studies, William wants to work in education and hopes one day to be a role model for

Sudanese children disabled by war—an inspiration, perhaps, for all children.

A good thing about Dinka people, they teach a child when he is very young what his name is, what his father's name is, his grandfather's, all the way back to the ten generations. So if he ever gets lost, he can say who he is, people will know, and they will return him. And just by the name, people will know what tribe, what area you are from.

SOMETIMES, WHETHER HE IS IN SUDAN or America, people ask him why he didn't return to his family's village after he escaped captivity. Patiently, William answers that he was a runaway slave. Someone's property. People would hunt for him; it was too dangerous to try to go home. Also, as a captive, he had been forced to walk at night, so he would have had no idea what direction to go in, where home even was.

And sometimes, though he rarely speaks of it or asks for help, people ask him about his disability.

People treat you differently when you have a disability. I don't blame them. When they ask how it happened or what happened, I have two different answers. The first answer I just say, "An accident." Then they don't ask any more about it. The second answer I say, "It's a long story." And they drop it.

With my family, my disability makes me nervous. I left when I was six years old, lose my arm and my fingers, then I go back. It's not hurting me because I've been dealing with it for so many years—what is it, twelve, thirteen years now? Since I was nineteen years old. But when I go home, I'm handicapped. My mom's seeing me, my dad's seeing me, my other grandmother's seeing me, a lot of the rest of the people are seeing me, and there are a lot of tears, crying, sadness. It's hard for them. I'm nervous, seeing

*my family so sad. And it's Dinka culture, so they try to please me.
I wake up, do everything I know how to do for myself, but they're
right there, trying to do everything for me because I'm handicapped. I start to feel, oh, I didn't see I was handicapped before,
but now with them all trying to be there, doing this and this and
this for me, I feel I am handicapped even more.*

*When my daughter first asked about my arm and my hand,
what happened to me, I told her about my factory accident in
Cairo. "I'm sorry, Daddy. I love you," she said, then hugged me
for a long time. It hit me really hard then, that my daughter loves
me so much.*

*A lot of people in Sudan are disabled because of the war. Since
I'm disabled too, I understand their needs.*

WILLIAM MAWWIN CAME INTO MY LIFE in 2005, sitting,
unobserved, beneath a tree in my backyard during a party.
When he calls me Mom now, I am strong enough, changed
enough, trusting enough, to answer with Son. The early
doubts I had about this stranger's motives—was his loyalty
feigned or genuine?—have gone. William long ago proved his
credibility, his integrity, to me. My two daughters, initially
baffled, annoyed by the idea of a grown "brother," a stranger
they did not know and did not choose, are quick and proud
to call William their brother. He is a member of our family,
and when we celebrate birthdays, weddings, holidays, none of
these occasions feel complete without him. He attends events
I am involved in and has spoken to students in my classes. A
charismatic speaker, he tells his story without embellishment
or self-pity. I have watched professors and students alike pay
rapt attention, then ask William questions with tears in their
eyes. Self-reliant, William rarely complains or asks for anything, but if he does, if he needs money for some unexpected
or extra expense, I know the request comes with difficulty,

that he hates asking and has exhausted every other possibility. At times, he expresses anger and disillusionment over a local nonprofit organization that invited him to speak more than twenty times on its behalf between 2003 and 2011. He raised money for the organization at these speaking engagements, yet was paid almost nothing, and the five-hundred-dollar scholarship he had been assured he would receive as compensation was never awarded to him. It is an old pattern, being cheated of what he is owed, bitterly reminiscent of his life as a slave. Yet if anyone in my family needs William, he will find his way to that person, without a car, without money—invariably, loyally, he shows up.

Our family celebrated Thanksgiving as I was in the midst of writing William's story. After dinner, I asked him if I might try taking a few photographs of him specifically for this article. I imagined one photo of his scarred upper back, another of him facing the camera, wearing his dress shirt and russet corduroy jacket. I was a bit unsure, a little embarrassed to ask, but when I did, William good-naturedly agreed. In front of my older daughter, my son-in-law, and me, he took his jacket and shirt off. Half naked, he turned boyish, joking around, mugging for the camera. When I asked about the long, faded scar in the center of his chest, he answered that it was from a knife blade that had been heated in a fire, then held against his chest. "People ask if I've had heart surgery when they see that scar," he laughed.

The lighting was wrong in the room, the photos turned out badly, and the whole idea, I realized, after William had gone home, had been a bit melodramatic anyway. As my daughter and I worked quietly in the kitchen, cleaning up, washing and putting away dishes, she stopped suddenly.

"Now I know how he gets dressed. I've always wondered."

"What do you mean?"

"Mom, didn't you see? To do the buttons on his shirt, to get dressed, William uses his teeth."

Surrounded by the remnants of a holiday feast, its store-bought bounty, we stood a moment, saying nothing.

My life, it teaches me to watch, to not get upset or excited too much. When I'm upset, I'm only making it worse. I have to breathe every day, I have to think of the next day. If I get too excited, there is no one to rescue me, I am on my own. I have to think what is good and bad. I have to watch. Take my time. Imitate people when they aren't watching. I learned that good people can turn to bad people. When someone wants something from you, they treat you nice until they get what they want. That is the reality, but I don't want to treat people like that. I appreciate all the people who did good things to me. I even appreciate the ones who did bad things to me. I really wish I could sit down with every one of those people, show them my appreciation, show forgiveness. I wish I could do that.

WILLIAM MAWWIN IS NOW thirty-four years old. Named Manyuol at birth, renamed Ali by his Arab master, baptized William after a fourteenth-century Scottish warrior by an Italian priest, William speaks Dinka, Arabic, and English. He became an American citizen on July 17, 2009, began to attend Scottsdale Community College full-time, and in 2010 began receiving assistance in the form of federal disability payments and federal Pell Grants. On May 10, 2013, William received his associate's degree in business from Scottsdale Community College, and this fall he will begin his junior year at Arizona State University, working toward a BS in global agribusiness. He intends to use his American education to return and help the government and the people of South Sudan.

After his graduation, William Mawwin told me he was going

to reclaim his birth name, inherited from nine generations of grandfathers and tribal chiefs. One of these grandfathers, Manyuol Mawein, eight feet tall and blessed with thousands of cattle, many wives, dozens of children, remains a legendary figure among the Dinka.

Having survived slavery, imprisonment, amputation, and nearly thirty years of exile, William, no longer a male child believed dead, no longer a "ghost father," now knows who he is: a direct descendant of Dinka chiefs, generations of men named Manyuol, whose tribal leadership was marked by gentleness, dignity, and a just, visionary wisdom.

William—Manyuol Mawein—has come home.

Circle of Friends

ONE RAINY MORNING LAST MAY, I stood beneath my cheap, black tourist umbrella in the middle of Trafalgar Square, bereft of direction or desire. My life suddenly felt hollow, my writer's solitude a barbed loneliness.

In Arizona a few days before, my youngest daughter had gotten married, and on the day she left for her honeymoon, a long-distance relationship I derived thin but familiar comfort from abruptly ended. Determined to try to celebrate this new independence, I'd given myself a week in London. Instead, an excess of freedom gathered itself into a hard burst of loneliness in Trafalgar Square. Shorn of love, stripped of family, ambushed by sadness and dangerously close to self-pity, I stood as if paralyzed, fractured by loss.

> And you? When will you begin that long journey into yourself?
>
> —Rūmī

The ancient Latin root for *pilgrim* is *per agrum*, one who walks beyond known boundaries; pilgrimage derives from the Latin *pelegrinus*—a foreigner or wayfarer who journeys to a holy place, sacred center, or natural setting imbued with spirit. Going on pilgrimage, the wayfarer hopes to receive healing—exactly what her spirit requires. Typically, the "call" to travel outside the familiar comes as a person finds herself at an impasse, in soul crisis, though it is up to her to say *yes* and go.

During my week in London, the call to pilgrimage came by way of an unexpected introduction to Carol Beckwith and Angela Fisher, renowned photographers of African tribes. A mutual friend, paleoanthropologist Don Johanson, learning I was in town, asked me to join them for a country weekend in Norfolk. Over Sunday breakfast, Carol and Angela expressed warm interest in my writing and in my mentorship of a South Sudanese college student, William Mawwin. When they suggested I accompany them in September on a ten-day trip down the Omo River in Ethiopia, I thought it a fantastic, exotic invitation, impossible to accept. I would have to take time away from work, I reasoned. The cost would be exorbitant. Still, if it seemed irrational, even reckless, to travel to Ethiopia, the alternative, an empty house, the parade of long, silent hours, seemed unbearable. Plundering my savings, making no formal announcement of my departure, desperate for distraction, alert to any chance for wisdom, I leaped into the unknown.

A SHORT, STEEP RISE UP FROM THE OMO RIVER, Camp Lumale is tucked within a sun-splashed grove of majestic, broadleafed fig trees, leaves rustling as agile black-and-white colobus monkeys swing from branch to branch to peer down upon new arrivals hiking wearily up from their small boat to a clean row of canvas tents. I have not camped in a tent since I was a stick-limbed tomboy with scabbed elbows and knees, a "holy terror" sent by my exhausted parents to a place called Camp Talawanda. Now, I stand in front of a khaki tent with a canvas-floored foyer and zippered entrance. On one side of me is an outdoor cedar table with canvas chair, on the other, a standing canvas "sink" filled with clean water. A tiny, rectangular mirror dangles off a tent pole. Mosquitoes zing around my face as I unzip the tent, crouch in. A twin bed, a second table, and beneath it, a fat, red spray can labeled *doom*. That first night, I lie awake, listening to the river's throaty murmur, the raucous cries of baboons echoing up and down the riverbank, thrillingly close.

Mornings, our motorized boat takes us up- or downstream, the broad, taupe river bearing us past arid, chalky landscapes, heavily forested areas, scythed clearings. The river's odor, heavy, clinging, vegetal, combines with the smell of fire and drifting white smoke. Families are working small plots of land, burning off brush and trees, planting broad beans, maize, and sorghum, a grain used in porridge, beer, and bread. We pass goliath herons, solitary Nile crocodiles slithering off muddy banks into the river, herds of cattle treading down worn paths to drink, women filling large plastic jerricans with river water to rope to their backs or carry on their heads back to their villages. Resting against the riverbank like narrow, split seedpods are long fishing boats made from hollowed-out logs. As our boat motors along, individuals and whole families, attracted by the sound, appear along embankments, on the edges of clearings, or in silhouette along cliffs. Their hands float up in an unhurried gesture of peaceful greeting; the children wave excitedly or simply stare. Time moves differently here, I think, raising my hand in response. Life is aligned with seasons, cycles, stars—everything part of some elaborate, measureless design.

> The life of a man is a circle from childhood to childhood . . .
>
> —Black Elk

In the Kara, Hamar, and Nyangatom villages we visit, thatched homes and granaries, even branch-woven pens for sheep and goats, are circular. Ceremonies—courtship dances, rites of passage—move in circles. Even the calabashes, dried gourds used as bowls for sorghum porridge or to drink honey beer or "coffee" made from tan hulls of coffee beans, are round. Abstractly, a circle represents infinity, completion, no beginning and no end; the world I live in is formed of squares, grids, intersections, sharp angles. These tribal people live much as their ancestors did thousands of years ago, within expanding circles of homes and villages, beneath moving spheres of sun and moon, even as they drink and fish from and oar in rough-carved trees down the Omo River.

> It is important to make a record of African cultural tradition before it disappears. This is what drives us to record as much of the richness and beauty of these cultures as possible, for future generations of Africans as well as for the outside world.
>
> —Angela Fisher

Angela and Carol's first journey to the remote Omo River region, part of the Great Rift Valley, was in 1985. On this trip, they carry three digital cameras apiece, hung around their necks, strapped across their shoulders, semipermanent extensions of their bodies. The running conversation between them is a specialized language of apertures, speed, brackets, lenses, light. They take hundreds of shots each day, continually adjusting to contrasts in light, composition. Positioning themselves for a shot, each becomes utterly still, emptied of self, and in a single, perfect click, captures the essence of a Nyangatom mother, stitching a goatskin skirt, her hair coiled and glistening with red clay and animal fat; a group of Kara children playing on a rise above the river, bodies ghost-streaked with white clay, blooms of water hyacinth or pink desert rose in their hair; or Nyangatom men mixing water with white or yellow clay, ornamenting one another's tall, lean bodies with zigzags, stripes, circles—vivid, dissolvable geometries.

I ask Carol and Angela over camp breakfast one morning whether they have regrets, having never married, had children, led a more "conventional" life. I ask, too, about their friendship, decades long, stronger than most marriages I know.

"A lot of people do assume we're lesbians," Angela answers. "But we've been proposed to several times, and we have boyfriends. As for regrets, no. In the end, you listen to your heart and find you want to go on doing exactly what you are doing."

"Our experience of nearly forty years in Africa," Carol adds, "has been like living in an all-encompassing narrative ritual. We keep pushing boundaries, and what we do is consumed by passion. The two of us do have this amazing bond, as well as a similar aesthetic about body art, jewelry, rites, and ceremonies."

I ask about future plans.

"We have no five-year plan," says Angela with a smile. "We've each had close brushes with death. Four-and-a-half years ago, Carol nearly died in a plane crash in Nairobi. So we now feel it is important to live fully, completely, in the moment. Our biggest project is completing our archive, a record of birth-to-death ceremonies covering the entire continent of Africa."

The Traveler's Lamp

One of the oldest symbols of pilgrimage is the "traveler's lamp," said to light the way within as well as the road ahead. Near the end of our ten days on the Omo River, Carol and Angela reunite unexpectedly with Dore, a Kara man they first photographed in 1985 for their books *African Ark* and *Painted Bodies*. The reunion is joyous, and they invite Dore to dine with us in camp that night. Walking from his village of Dus, he arrives late, a tall, elegant man wrapped in a long, traditional blanket, a clay skullcap with a single white feather on his head. When he is done eating, Carol opens her iPad, the modern-day traveler's lamp, and sets it in front of him. We draw our chairs close to watch a short documentary spliced from Carol and Angela's two previous visits to the Omo region nearly thirty years before. Under a wide cloudless sky, young Kara men, ceremonially painted for courtship, sing and dance. Dore sees himself, recognizes his friends, some, he says, no longer living. He calls out their names—American, Zeno—and in a gesture of profound emotion, presses his hand again and again to his heart. On the iPad's screen, Dore's youth is restored, preserved in some media eternity. Sitting beside me in the darkness, Dore is a dignified old man, many of his friends gone.

That September night, sheltered within a grove of fig trees, the Omo River nearby, I understand that I am an infinitesimal, essential part of the human family. Included, encircled, temporary.

On holy ground.

Note: *The peoples of this once-remote region of Africa are under imminent threat of extinction. International investment and development, the seizing of traditional grazing lands and forests for commercial cotton and sugarcane plantations, and the completion of a series of massive, hydroelectric dams are endangering these tribes and their way of life. For more information on Carol Beckwith and Angela Fisher, and to find out how to help, please see: www.africanceremonies.com*

On Bibliomancy, Anthropodermic Bibliopegy, and the Eating Papers; or, Proust's Porridge

Bibliomancy: divination by means of a book opened at random to a verse or passage

I HAVE BEEN PACKING IN EARNEST, the sedimentia of four generations, strata of decades, the weight stone of things rolling away. I have sold, given away, disposed of by means of alleyway, obliging friends, strangers, and the Army that Saves, a third of my possessions. Another third has vanished into that public holding cube, the mini–storage unit. Contracting from 3,000 to 750 square feet of living space requires an epic purge. Mostly, I welcome it, but for one room, a room I resist to the last. My library, my carapace, my identity: writer. A room with a view, three desks, one thousand books, and a reading chair decimated by the dog. Two of the desks have already gone, leaving the third, not a desk at all but a rough-made pine table. The sad looking chair has been carted off to the upholsterer's. All that remains is books collected over a lifetime. Inherited, purchased, received as gifts, books signed by their authors, books stolen (my older sister's college paperback copy of Hardy's *Tess of the d'Urbervilles*; a 1959 copy of *Le Point*, "Univers de Proust," poached from a flat on rue

Blanche in Paris; a copy of E. J. Bellocq's *Storyville Portraits*, never returned to the Taos Library), dilapidated hardback books from my father's navy-brat youth (*Robinson Crusoe, The Last of the Mohicans, Robin Hood,* 200 More Tricks You Can Do). From my mother's Chicago girlhood (*Linda Lane's Adventures; Oriole's Adventures: Four Complete Adventure Books for Girls in One Big Volume; Daddy-Long-Legs*). A slim dark-blue-and-gold-lettered book, *SNAG 56,* about my grandfather's captaincy of a British hospital in World War II, books from friends, from auditioning lovers. Each book has had a place on my shelves. Now I am pulling them down, striking the set. This private library of paper, ink, and dust, these one thousand books in loose, friendly order, is the closest thing to an honest portrait of my life.

How to proceed? I call my publisher in Brooklyn, whose four-story brownstone feels entirely constructed of and held together by books, the air like old mucilage, tinged with shellac, rabbit glue. She suggests I break the process down, ask myself is this a book I could readily find another copy of, does it have sentimental value? If the former, let go, if the latter, keep. Armed with this system, I begin to sort and divide books into boxes. Initially tentative, indecisive, I turn discriminating, gimlet eyed, ruthless. First to go are books I feel indifferent to, then ones I loathe but have kept out of guilt or a sense of obligation. Eight boxes go to the Perryville Women's Correctional Facility, three to my house sitter, also a writer, seventeen to the storage catacomb, to be shuttered into the rented silence of a metal unit, stacked beside a job lot of Christmas ornaments, children's toys, old linens, incomplete silver sets, stacks of furniture, and three centuries of family albums. The remaining books will be my companions in a narrow room with a pine writing table and a reading chair reclaimed by the dog.

IN THE ART OF BIBLIOMANCY, one allows the pages of a book considered sacred to fall open to a random passage. The Greeks divined wisdom from Homer's *Iliad*. Virgil's *Aeneid* was used for divination during medieval times, the *I Ching* is a current favorite with bibliomancers. There is a Web site devoted to literary bibliomancy, bibliomancy.org, "the wisdom of the ages at your fingertips." Enter the site with your life question, receive a reply from Dickens, Dostoyevsky, Virgil, Hermann Hesse, Homer, etc. Type the question into a box, select a book from the list, and the answer, intended as insight, appears. I ask Charles Dickens about my future and receive this from *Great Expectations*, passage 406 of 1550:

> Biddy turned her face suddenly towards mine, and looked far more attentively at me than she had looked at the sailing ships. "It was neither a true nor a very polite thing to say," she remarked, directing her eyes to the ships again. "Who said it?" I was disconcerted, for I had broken away without quite seeing where I was going to. It was not to be shuffled off now, however, and I answered, "The beautiful young lady at Miss Havisham's, and she's more beautiful than anybody ever was, and I admire her dreadfully, and I want to be a gentleman on her account." Having made this lunatic confession, I began to throw my torn-up grass into the river, as if I had some thoughts of following it.

I might have consulted Jane Austen, George Sand, Colette, or Mavis Gallant, but none of them are on the list. My diviners are solidly male.

As I relegate one thousand volumes to their fates, I ease my book ache with an invented subset of bibliomancy:

epigraphancy. Choosing books at random, I flip to their epigraphs for more insights into my vague future.

Not every book contains an epigraph; a few have three or four. Epigraphs lend smart style, outfitting the author in witty, philosophic, or enigmatic dress. They also offer the reader a set of jeweled binoculars through which to view the distant stage, draw back curtains on the opening scene.

Here are random epigraphancies to reflect upon as I take slow leave of my private library, my Joseph's coat of many books, their ivory, deckle edged, or smooth pages tattooed with ink both sumptuous and plain:

> An oasis of horror in a desert of boredom.
>
> —Charles Baudelaire
> (Roberto Bolaño, *2666*)

> My dear, these things are life.
>
> —George Meredith
> (Mercè Rodoreda, *The Time of the Doves*)

> Novels arise out of the shortcomings of history.
>
> —F. von Hardenberg, later Novalis
> *Fragmente und Studien*, 1799–1800
> (Penelope Fitzgerald, *The Blue Flower*)

> I am accustoming myself to the idea of regarding every sexual act as a process in which four persons are involved. We shall have a lot to discuss about that.
>
> —Sigmund Freud, *Letters*
> (Lawrence Durrell, *Justine*)

Anthropodermic Bibliopegy:
the practice of binding books in human skin

Stones, clay and wood tablets, bamboo, papyrus, silk, bone, bronze, shell, palm leaf, flax linen—the earliest writing surfaces. Rolled scrolls with wood handles on either end, scrolls folded like a concertina, "butterfly" scrolls bound on one edge, codices—the earliest books. (Jack Kerouac's *On the Road*, written in three weeks as a scroll manuscript, without punctuation, was recently republished in its original form.) During the first century AD in China, the earliest known paper was made from a mixture of mulberry, fishnet, and hemp waste. In the third century AD, a writing surface known as parchment began to be made from the skins of asses, antelope, sheep, cattle, pig, deer, horse, camel. Parchment consists mainly of collagen, and the highest-quality parchment, vellum, or *veau*, was made from calfskin. Finer still was uterine vellum made from the skin of stillborn or unborn calves. A vein network appearing in a piece of vellum was termed a "veining of the sheet."

From the fourteenth century, the most valuable books and documents were written on vellum. Due to its rarity and expense, monastery parchments were often scrubbed and written over, leaving faint traces of the previous writing, a holy palimpsest of gospels ghosting beneath a medieval sermon.

Early writing instruments made of bone or bronze marked moist clay tablets. Reed brushes were used to write on scrolls of papyrus, and the Romans used metal styluses to press Latin letters onto sheets of wax supported by tablets of beech or fir. Around 600 AD, the quill pen was invented in Seville. Long wing feathers of swans, turkeys, geese, crows, owls, hawks, and eagles were plucked, cleaned, sharpened, and dipped in ink, filling the hollow shaft or reservoir of the feather. Not until the eighteenth century was a machine-made, steel pen point mass produced.

The first inks were made from wood smoke and oil thickened with gelatin from asses' skins and musk. Sulfate and gallnuts produced iron-gall ink, tannic acid and iron salts, bound by resin, another. Tar, carbon, oil, honey, gum, the stuff of early script. Brown-black dye from cuttlefish, too, and purple ink from squid, scarlet from madder, and from scale insects named Kermez vermilio and cochineal. Indigo ink was made from a mixture of woad, indigo, and gallnuts; books were bound with glue made from boiled rabbit skins, fish, horses. (Secret or "invisible" ink, made from lemon juice, milk, vinegar starch, urine, etc., is a subtributary of ink history, filled with tales of wartime espionage, prison breaks, covert love letters, and children's mischief.) The Declaration of Independence was written on animal membrane, as parchment is now called—a term that actually encompasses both parchment and vellum. At the university where I teach, every classroom is required to have a copy of the Declaration of Independence, printed on faux parchment, tacked to its walls. The original Declaration of Independence, Bill of Rights, United States Constitution, and Articles of Confederation were all inscribed on the flayed, scraped, pumiced, and chalked skins of calves.

Ink from fish, grubs, plants, soot. Clay, stone, dried leaves, plants, silk, animal skins. Feathers engorged with ink. A yearning for permanence.

In our tenure on this planet, we have moved from organic to inorganic materials, from writing with earth's substances to writing electronically, with light. Scudding upon iClouds, bathed in iLight, the evocation *i* underscoring our devotion not to the planet, but to our disembodied, immortal hoped-for selves.

In my skin are the prayers and all the blessings made to Holy Church.

And have not calves, goats, kids, Coneys, hares and cats skin? As vellum, they may be well written on. To be sure, their parchment is worth more than your skin, which serves you less.

—Dialogue between two French monks,
fifteenth century
(Ronald Reed, *The Making and Nature of Parchment*)

In reading about the distinctions between parchment and vellum, animal versus vegetable vellum, I stumble upon a term unknown to me—*anthropodermic bibliopegy*—the practice of binding books with human skin. My morbid reading self plunges on.

In 2007, a book entitled *A True and Perfect Relation of the Whole Proceedings against the Late Most Barbarous Traitors Garnet a Jesuit and his Confederates*, bound in the skin of Father Henry Garnet, a faint impression of his death mask on its cover, was sold by an anonymous collector to an anonymous buyer at auction for $11,000. While Father Garnet did not participate in the 1605 Gunpowder Plot to blow up the Houses of Parliament and assassinate King James I (now celebrated on November 5 as Guy Fawkes Day), the Jesuit priest willingly heard the confessions of those who were involved. Guilty by implication, Garnet was drawn, quartered, and a portion of his skin used to bind the account of legal proceedings against him.

Housed among other medical oddities at Old Surgeons' Hall in Edinburgh is a worn, unremarkable-looking pocket book. Brownish-black with a pebbled texture, it is embossed with faded gilt lettering: EXECUTED 28 JAN 1829 BURKE'S SKIN POCKETBOOK. The pocket book, empty of pages, used for personal notes and money, is bound in the skin of notorious criminal William Burke, who, along with William Hare, his accomplice, murdered sixteen people, selling the corpses of their victims to Dr. Robert Knox to be used for dissections in his highly popular anatomy lessons. Burke was hanged for the murders, and his body was (ironically) dissected at Edinburgh Medical College, his skin used to bind this otherwise common-looking pocket book.

The practice of binding books in human skin began at least in the sixteenth century and waned in the latter years of the Victorian age, the same era that memorialized loved ones with "jewelry" fashioned from the often abundant, shorn hair of the deceased. Books were bound in human skin for diverse reasons, including to memorialize, as a gift to loved ones, or to bind court testimonies against criminals in their own punished hides.

Human skin, tanned, looks indistinguishable from goat, cattle, and sheep but for variance in pore size, shape, and a peculiar waxy odor. The tanning process destroys DNA, making it difficult to differentiate between skins of human, goat, cow, and pig, but a new technique, Peptide Mass Fingerprinting, or PMF, has proven useful in determining whether a book claiming to be bound in human skin through inscription or questionable historical "evidence" is genuine. In 1935, a book was deposited in Harvard's Houghton Library by book collector John B. Stetson Jr. and given to the library in 1954 by Stetson's widow. In April 2014, this book, Arsène Houssaye's *Des destinées de l'ame* (*On the Destiny of the Soul*), was determined through PMF to be bound in human skin. "The PMF from *Des destinées de l'ame* matched the human reference, and clearly eliminated other common parchment sources such as sheep, cattle, and goat," Bill Lane, director of Harvard's Mass Spectrometry and Proteomics Resource Laboratory and Daniel Kirby of the Straus Center for Conservation and Technical Studies reported to the Houghton Library blog.

Sometime in the 1880s, Houssaye had given his book, a

meditation on the soul and life after death, to his friend Dr. Ludovic Bouland, an ardent bibliophile. Dr. Bouland bound *Des destinées de l'ame* using skin from the back of an unclaimed female mental patient who had died of a stroke. A note penned by the doctor, inserted within the pages of the book, reads, "This book is bound in human skin parchment on which no ornament has been stamped to preserve its elegance. By looking carefully, you easily distinguish pores of the skin. A book about the human soul deserved to have a human covering. I had kept this piece of human skin taken from the back of a woman."

The female binding of *Des destinées de l'ame*, as reported by the *Harvard Crimson*, has a "greenish-gold hue as well as visible pores."

In the late nineteenth century, a French countess, dying of tuberculosis, requested that a strip of skin from her shoulders be delivered upon her death to writer and astronomer Camille Flammarion, so that he might use her skin in the binding of his next book. Compliant, perhaps flattered, Flammarion bound his 1877 copy of *Les Terres du Ciel*, *The Lands of the Sky*, a description of the planets in our solar system, with the countess' shoulder skin. Until 1925, the book was displayed in a library in Juvisy-sur-Orge, France.

A nineteenth-century English book binder of erotica used the breasts of deceased females, purchased from medical interns, to bind copies of *Justine and Juliette* by Donatien Alphonse François, better known as the Marquis de Sade, and in London's Wellcome Library, a seventeenth-century book on virginity, Séverin Pineau's *De virginitatis notis, graviditate et partu*, is currently on view, rebound in human hide and tanned with sumac by the same Dr. Ludovic Bouland.

This grisly legend persists: When Marie-Thérèse of Savoy-Carignan, Princess de Lamballe, an intimate of Marie

Antoinette's, was executed in 1792, her naked corpse was pulled through the streets and the skin from her thighs removed to be used for the binding of a book. In whose private collection stands this rumored book, neatly bound in the marmoreal pallor of the Princess de Lamballe's tender skin?

As Dr. Simon Chaplin, head of the Wellcome Library, says, "There may still be a number of books in libraries and private collections bound in human skin, not yet categorized or identified."

Each of us is a two-footed manuscript, a work in progress. Briefly bound in our own skin, uncataloged, unshelved, we form some seven billion volumes of the world's living library.

Within us too are digested libraries, cellular *bibliothèques* made of every book we have ever read. Writers fold sentences into crevices of the body, scratched in delible, sympathetic ink.

We are characters wandering, largely unaware, inside an inconceivably grand body of narrative, its scope greater than that of any novel by Balzac, Hugo, Sand, Dostoyevsky, or Tolstoy, the plot a biomorphic field, an Akashic record of all that has occurred and will occur.

If I kiss you, will you taste of all the books you have read or only the last one? If we are writers and we kiss, will we taste one another's unwritten, still dreamed books?

It ever was, and is, and shall be,
ever-living Fire, in measures being
kindled and in measures going out.

—Heraclitus
(Annie Dillard, *Pilgrim at Tinker Creek*)

The Eating Papers; or, Proust's Porridge

Visiting a friend in Paris, I read her copy of Larry Dossey's *Healing Beyond the Body: Medicine and the Infinite Reach of the Mind*, and learn that eating words inscribed on paper is an old, traditional folk cure for sickness.

When he became seriously ill at a conference in Baja, Dossey asked his friend Dr. Frank Lawlis to write words on a piece of paper and smash the paper into a capsule size that he could swallow with a glass of water. This would be his only medicine. He began to recover in three days, and though his friend considered the experiment a failure, since Dossey's symptoms lingered for weeks afterward, Dossey reasoned that had he not eaten his paper capsule, he might well have died.

As an elementary student at the Queen of Apostles Catholic school in Chicago, poet Jeanine Hathaway carefully wrote "aspirin" on the corner of a page from her notebook, tore it off, rolled it into a ball, and swallowed it. Faith worked. She felt instantly better, her sickness gone, as if she had taken a real aspirin minus the vinegar taste.

In France, Italy, Russia, and Germany, Bible verses, prayers, and spells were written down to be eaten as medicine—in Germany, these were called *Esszettel* or "eating papers." To drink these papers with water was to be cured by the power of words. In Holstein, the following words would be written on paper and given to a person with fever to be swallowed with water: "Fever stay away. (The person's name) is not at home." Reports from the fifteenth century describe apples being written upon and eaten, three almonds inscribed with words, squares of gingerbread imprinted with magical spells, and small pieces of buttered bread etched with a quill dipped in ink, to be eaten on three consecutive Fridays at sunrise and sundown. An epileptic might be helped by a formula written on a piece of paper using a needle that had once sewn something for a dead person, the paper then being warmed over steam from heated milk and presented to the epileptic on a piece of buttered bread. Even sick animals received *Esszettel* treatments. Today, a Bayer aspirin, a cross stamped on its round, white surface, is perceived by patients to be more effective than a smooth-faced, unadorned aspirin. And what of the Eucharist, believed by the Catholics who ingest it to be the literal body, the flesh of Jesus, healing the disease of sin, making them whole? What of the physician's scrawled medical prescription (℞ being Latin for "recipe"), legible only to the pharmacist—does it have shamanistic power? Is faith a greater medicine than medicine?

In the 1920s, documents found in Eastern Mongolia described the Tibetan folk-medicine cure of eating pieces of paper with healing words printed on them. Approximately one inch by one inch in size, the papers had prayers or spells written in Tibetan, with separate instructions in Mongolian for dosage or use.

In Uganda in the 1990s, photographs of a Christian charismatic preacher and healer were dissolved in water and drunk by his followers. In the Catholic tradition, images of the Madonna could be dissolved and drunk with water, or swallowed as pills.

BIBLIOPHAGY IS A RARE DISORDER wherein the afflicted person compulsively eats books. Symptoms include feelings of relief upon eating books, and a reduction in anxiety brought about by the eating of books. Treatment consists of behavior therapy and medication. But if words can be eaten as magic formulae, *Esszettel* to treat sickness, cannot whole books be prescriptively dined upon and digested? If I eat a page of Proust a day, scissored up and stirred into warm milk, a kind of porridge, will

Proust's words, his brain and style, over time, become part of my own? Might I compound a Virginia Woolf topical ointment, ingest two Shakespeare gelatin capsules before bed and again upon waking? Is there a Flaubert lozenge or troche? A smear of Chekhov for my buttered bread? Oh, dear Physician, will it add to the effectiveness of my long-term treatment, if I, poor ailing author, drink such august faces, snipped and floating, in water or better, wine?

MAY THESE WORDS, EATEN OR DRUNK, cure all straying thoughts:

> *Mos gus yod na*
> *Khyl so od tung.*

> Where there is veneration,
> Even a dog's tooth emits light.

—Tibetan proverb
(Lawrence Durrell, *The Black Book*)

Acknowledgments

F OR THEIR GRACE AND GENEROSITY, I thank David Morley;
Maureen Freely; Louise Doughty; Jewell Parker Rhodes;
Mother Ellen Monsees, RSCJ; Father Murray Bodo, OFM; Jeffrey Masson; Mario Materassi; Nirvana Ortese; Tim Schell;
Bryan Furuness; and my students at the University of Warwick—Anna, Robin, Leila, Taylor, Zigian, Suzanne, Amy, Victoria, Nate, Sarah, Laura, Mike. Gratitude to my first reader,
Noelle Pritchard; thanks also to Jess Barkley, Caitlin Pritchard,
Gabriel Rushing, Simon (star of "Doxology"), Clara Darby,
Bradford Morrow, David Shields, Peter Stitt, Robin Hemley,
Matt Bell, Christopher Merrill, Gregory Wolfe, Krista Katrovas, Richard Katrovas, Pam Uschuk, William Pitt Root, Cynthia Hogue, Drue Heinz, Kristy Davis, Sara Nelson, Sarah
Twombly, Anne McPeak, Retired Major General Walter D.
Givhan, Masha Hamilton, Connie May Fowler, Senior Airman
Ashton Goodman, Sandra White, David Flint, Mark Edward
Goodman, Chasity Goodman, William Akoi Mawwin, Steve
Lagerfeld, Darcy Courteau, John Milewski, Joe Lockard, Ayşe
Papatya Bucak, Carol Beckwith, Angela Fisher, Don Johanson,
Leslie Iwerks, Lale Biwa, the Omo River peoples of the Kara
(or Karo), Hamar and Nyangatom tribes, Luisa Materassi, Millicent Materassi, Gyorgyi Szabo, Susannah Casprini, Simona
Lumachelli, Giuditta Viceconte, Penelope Byrd, Jim Weaver,

Caleb, Leigh Flayton, Michael Crow, Judith Smith, Leigh Haber, Kristen Burt LaRue, Angela Dell, Brian Bender, Adam Reed, and my agent, Joy Harris.

Thanks to Sacred Heart Schools, Atherton, California; Vermont College; Recursos de Santa Fe, Santa Fe Community College; Arizona State University; the University of Warwick; Drue Heinz and the Hawthornden International Retreat for Writers; the University of Florence, Italy; the Center for American Studies, Rome; the Air Force Institute of Technology; the Virginia G. Piper Charitable Trust; and the Afghan Women's Writing Project's selfless mentors and brave writers.

Heartfelt thanks to the inestimable Erika Goldman and her team at Bellevue Literary Press: Leslie Hodgkins, Crystal Sikma, Joe Gannon, and Molly Mikolowski.

You have turned solitude and uncertainty into a rich collaboration.

I would like to thank the publications in which these essays appeared:

"A Room in London"
in *Changing Hands Bookstories*

"From the Deep South to the Desert South:
    An Epiphyte's Confession"
in *Clackamas Literary Review*

"On Kaspar Hauser"
in Barnes & Noble's "More In Store"

"Time and Biology: On the Threshold of the Sacred"
in *Patagonian Winds* as "The Ethics of Fiction"

"Elephant in the Dark"
in *Mooring Against the Tide: Writing Fiction and Poetry*

"The Gift of Warwick"
in *Marginalia: The Magazine of the Virginia G. Piper Center
for Creative Writing*

"Doxology"
in the *Gettysburg Review*; excerpt in
O, The Oprah Magazine

"A Solemn Pleasure"
in *Conjunctions* and *The Inevitable: Contemporary Writers
Confront Death*, W.W. Norton

"A Graven Space"
in *From the Faraway Nearby: Georgia O'Keeffe as Icon*

"Decomposing Articles of Faith"
in *On Earth As It Is*

"Finding Ashton"
in *O, The Oprah Magazine*

"'Still, God Helps You': Memories of a Sudanese Child Slave"
in the *Wilson Quarterly*

"Circle of Friends"
in *Arrive*

"On Bibliomancy, Anthropodermic Bibliopegy,
and the Eating Papers; Or, Proust's Porridge"
in *Conjunctions*